The Prince

Abigail Thorn

T0353283

methuen | drama

LONDON • NEW YORK • OXFORD • NEW DELHI • SYDNEY

METHUEN DRAMA
Bloomsbury Publishing Plc
50 Bedford Square, London, WC1B 3DP, UK
1385 Broadway, New York, NY 10018, USA
29 Earlsfort Terrace, Dublin 2, Ireland

BLOOMSBURY, METHUEN DRAMA and the Methuen
Drama logo are trademarks of Bloomsbury Publishing Plc

First published in Great Britain 2022

A catalogue record for this book is available from the British Library.

A catalog record for this book is available from the Library of Congress.

ISBN: PB: 978-1-3503-5237-7
ePDF: 978-1-3503-5238-4
eBook: 978-1-3503-5239-1

Series: Modern Plays

Typeset by Mark Heslington Ltd, Scarborough, North Yorkshire

To find out more about our authors and books visit
www.bloomsbury.com and sign up for our newsletters.

The Prince

Cast

Hotspur	**Abigail Thorn**
Lady Kate	**Tianna Arnold**
Sam	**Joni Ayton-Kent**
Jen	**Mary Malone**
Northumberland/	
King Henry IV	**Ché Walker**
Prince Hal	**Corey Montague-Sholay**
Worcester	**Richard Rees**
Douglas	**Tyler Luke Cunningham**

Creative team

Director	Natasha Rickman
Dramaturg	Donnacadh O'Briain
Writer	Abigail Thorn
Executive Producer	David Wiskus
Streaming Partners	Nebula
Producer	Simon Paris
Producer	George Warren
General Manager	Rae Lee
Associate Director/	
Movement Director	E.M Williams
Sound Designer/Composer	Rodent
Lighting & AV Designer	Martha Godfrey
Present-Day Costume &	
Set Designer	Lulu Tam
Historical Costume Designer	
& Supervisor	Rebecca Cartwright
Fight Director	Bethan Clark
Intimacy Director	Tigger Blaize
Casting Consultant &	
Trumpet Player	Harrison Knights
Dialect Coach	Nick Trumble
Electric Guitar Composer	
& Understudy	Frances Bolley

Hair & Make Up Designer	Nicki Buglewicz
Vocal Coach	Victoria Woodward
Costume Design Associate & Dresser	Asher Thomas
Production Managers	Andreas Ayling and Charlie Earl
Company Stage Manager	Lois Sime
Assistant Stage Manager	Paris Linxuan Wu
Press Agent	Madelaine Bennett
Marketing Manager	Natalie Yalden
Graphic Design/Artwork	Matthew Smith and Stephanos Afrikanos
Poster Photographer	Greg Veit
Filming (behind the scenes)	Mannbros, Timothy Mann and Ben Mann
Filming (theatre production)	Black Apron Entertainment, Daniel Bailey and Gino Green

Abigail Thorn – (She/Her) Writer and Lead – Hotspur

Abigail graduated drama school in 2017. In 2019 she made headlines by performing the complete works of Shakespeare 24/7 for five days, livestreamed over the Internet and raising $130,000 for Samaritans, alongside celebrity guests including Mara Wilson. Her stage credits include *Hamm* (RADA festival); *Thursday* (Southwark Playhouse) and *Much Ado About Nothing* (outdoor tour). Her screen credits include Django (Sky); *Ladhood* (BBC3) and *Chivalry* (Channel 4). As a writer she helped create *Immersive Dracula* (Electrowerkz), which sold out before being cut short by COVID. Abigail is also the creator of *Philosophy Tube*, a web-show with a global audience of over a million. She researches, writes, produces, directs and stars in every episode herself – *Vox* called her 2019 video *Men, Abuse, Trauma* 'one of the best TV episodes of the year.' In early 2021 Abigail came out publicly as 'one of Britain's most well-known trans women' (*Xtra Magazine*) – 'a woman who can do it all' (*Diva*). In her spare time, she also hosts the podcast Kill James Bond.

Tianna Arnold (They/Them) – Lady Kate

Tianna graduated Guildford School of Acting in 2021. Post-graduation they played Rosalind in *As You Like It* with Open Bar Theatre. They then secured their first screen role in the ITV series *Stonehouse* and also were a part of a couple rehearsed readings with Exeter Northcott Theatre and English touring theatre.

Joni Ayton-Kent (She/Her) – Sam

Joni is an actor and writer best known for playing Corporal Cheery in BBC America's *The Watch*. Other TV credits include *Don't Forget the Driver* (BBC Two) and *The Romanoffs* (Amazon). Stage credits include *Carousel* (Regent's Park

Open Air Theatre); *Revolt. She Said. Revolt Again* (The Other Room) and *Sweet Charity* (Donmar Warehouse).

Mary Malone (She/Her) – Jen

Mary Malone is an actor and theatre maker based in London, and a recent graduate from the Acting and Contemporary Theatre (CT) Course at East15 School of Acting. Her recent credits include: *The Jacket* a BBC arts film; *Safe* a digital theatre piece by Alexis Gregory and *Theatre For Two*, a touring immersive theatre experience with Kilter Theatre Company. Mary also appeared in Sky Arts' *Play in a Day* as Becca, directed by Josie Rourke.

Ché Walker (He/Him) – Northumberland/ King Henry IV

Ché Walker's writing includes: *Been So Long* (1998); *Flesh Wound* (Royal Court, winner of both George Devine Award, Arts Council Writer of the Future Award 2003). *Crazy Love* – for Paines Plough Theatre – was the winner of the Blanche Marvin Award in 2007.

In 2008, Ché made theatrical history with *The Frontline*, the first contemporary-set new play to be performed at Shakespeare's Globe in London. In 2009 his musical adaptation of *Been So Long* premiered at the Young Vic. The feature film adaptation of *Been So Long* was produced by Greenacre Films, the British Film Institute and Film 4, opening the London Film Festival in 2018, and broke all records for Netflix purchasing a UK film. *The 8th* – in collaboration with UK rock musician Paul Heaton – played the Manchester International Festival, The Barbican, Latitude Festival and toured nationwide.

Lovesong, in collaboration with UK soul legend Omar MBE, was produced by the English Touring Theatre in 2010. *The Lightning Child* (2013) made history as the first musical at Shakespeare's Globe. *Klook's Last Stand* (later re-titled *The Ballad of Klook and Vinette*) premiered at Park Theatre 2014 before playing at the NAMT festival in New York; Horizon Theatre, Atlanta; Red

Mountain Theatre, Birmingham, Alabama; Zach Theatre, Austin, Texas. *The Etienne Sisters* played the Theatre Royal Stratford East in 2015. *Time Is Love* played the Stella Adler Theatre, Los Angeles and the Finborough Theatre, London in 2019. *Wolf Cub* played Hampstead Theatre in 2022 and won nominations for Best Play, Director, Actor and Sound Design Off West End Awards. *My Old Flame* was directed by Academy Award Winner Asif Kapadia and screened on Channel 4. Ché has written and directed four short films which have won two awards and twenty-two film festival selections worldwide to date. Ché's feature documentary *Connie* has been selected for the Cork Indie Festival, Women of the Lens Festival 2022. As director, he has forty-three professional theatre credits both in US and London; as actor, he has forty professional TV and film credits and fifteen professional theatre credits.

Ché is an associate teacher at the Royal Academy of Dramatic Art (RADA), where he also sits on the audition panel. He has taught acting at Lamda, Central, East15, Webber Douglas, Stella Adler, Los Angeles for four years.

Corey Montague Sholay (He/Him) – Prince Hal

Corey Montague Sholay trained at the Bristol Old Vic Theatre School. Theatre credits include: *The Trumpet and the King* (Terra Nova Productions); *Bacon* (Finborough Theatre); *Wendy & Peter Pan* (Leeds Playhouse); *She Stoops to Conquer* and *As You Like It* (Guildford Shakespeare Company); *The Whip* and *King John* (Royal Shakespeare Company); *This Island's Mine* (King's Head Theatre); *Henry V* (Shakespeare at The Tobacco Factory); *The Enchanted* (The Bunker); *Normal* (Rift Theatre/Styx); *Snow White* (Sixteenfeet Productions); *The Hotel Cerise* (Theatre Royal Stratford East); *Little Revolution* and *ICU* (Almeida Theatre) and *Carpe Diem* (National Theatre). Short film credits include: *Kite Strings*, *Angry Face*, *Callum*, *Our Night* and *Home*.

Richard Rees (He/Him) – Worcester

Theatre credits include: *Pah-La* (Royal Court); *The Jew of Malta*, *Love's Sacrifice*, *Volpone*, *Snow in Midsummer* (RSC); *The Love Girl and the Innocent* (Southwark Playhouse); *#aiww: The Arrest of Ai Weiwei* (Hampstead Theatre); *Sixty-six Books* (Bush); *Love the Sinner* (National Theatre); *Another Paradise* (Kali); *Cinderella*, *Tears of the Indians*, *Twelfth Night* (Southampton Nuffield); *Three Sisters*, *Queen of Spades and I* (Orange Tree); *Little Red Riding Hood*, *World's Apart* (Stratford East); *M Butterfly* (Shaftesbury); *The Taming of the Shrew*, *Antony and Cleopatra* (Theatr Clwyd/Theatre Royal, Haymarket); *A Midsummer Night's Dream*, *The Merry Wives of Windsor*, *Twelfth Night*, *Bashville* (Regent's Park Open Air Theatre); *Measure for Measure* (Manchester Royal Exchange); *The White Devil*, *The Way of the World*, *The Seagull*, *Semi-Monde*, *Vautrin* (Glasgow Citizens); *Under Milk Wood* (Worcester).

Television credits include: *Law and Order*, *Silent Witness*, *Do Not Be Afraid*, *Pinochet's Progress*, *In The Beginning*, *Eastenders*, *Crossing The Line*, *Death On Everest*, *Bugs*, *The Healer*, *Red Eagle*.

Film credits include: *The Art of Love*, *Vacant Possession*, *The Omen*, *Aberdeen*, *Darklands*, *On Dangerous Ground*.

Tyler Luke Cunningham (He/Him) – Douglas

Tyler's professional career began in 2016 when he was cast in the hit TV show *Boy Meets Girl*. His other screen credits include *Holby City*, *I May Destroy You*, *Flack* and *Spider-Man Far From Home*.

On stage Tyler has performed at the Royal Albert Hall, Theatre Royal Stratford East, the Hackney Empire, Millfield Theatre, Soho Theatre and many more throughout the UK. When he's not performing professionally, Tyler is a partner in Write2Speak, a young and successful company that creates and delivers spoken work poetry workshops to people of all ages and all walks of life, further information is available via their website https://write2speak.co.uk.

Natasha Rickman (She/Her) – Director

As director, previous theatre credits include *Antigone* (Storyhouse); *Little Women* (Grosvenor Park Open Air Theatre); *Much Ado About Nothing* (RADA and Utah Shakespeare Festival); *The Duchess of Malfi*, *Romeo and Juliet*, *The Merry Wives of Whatsapp* (Creation Theatre); *The Snow Queen* (Iris Theatre); *The Time Machine* (site specific at the London Library for Creation Theatre); *A Christmas Carol* (Guildford Shakespeare Company and Jermyn Street Theatre); *The Last Fire Breathing Tunnel Digger*, online as part of Telling Tales (Muck and Rumble – Oncom finalists 2020); *Twelfth Night* (Rose Playhouse); *Rhino* (King's Head); *Hilda and Virginia* (Jermyn Street); *The Story Chef* (WhizzFizzFest) and shorts performed at The Royal Court, Southwark Playhouse and Park Theatre.

As associate/assistant director credits include *Romeo and Juliet* (The Globe); *The Comedy of Errors* (RSC); *A Little Night Music* (Storyhouse) and *Shirley Valentine* (Theatre Royal, Bury St Edmunds).

Natasha was artistic associate at Jermyn Street Theatre from 2017 until 2022 during their move to become a producing house. She is a freelance text and acting tutor for RADA, co-founded Women@ RADA which ran a series of rehearsed readings, and is a core ensemble member with The Faction.

Donnacadh O'Briain (He/Him) – Dramaturg

Donnacadh is an award-winning director and dramaturg. As director, productions have played at the Royal Shakespeare Company, in the West End, and internationally. Recent productions include *Operation Mincemeat* (Southwark Playhouse); *We Like To Move It Move It* (touring – also co-writer) and *Saviour* (Jermyn Street – also dramaturg). His acclaimed production of *Rotterdam* by Jon Brittain won the Olivier Award for Outstanding Achievement in an Affiliate Theatre, it subsequently ran at the Arts Theatre (West End) and toured the UK. Other productions include *Mother Christmas* (Hampstead Theatre); *Electrolyte* (Wildcard, Edinburgh/UK tour), and *Always Orange* by Fraser Grace (RSC), which reopened The Other Place Theatre in Stratford-upon-Avon. He is currently developing several projects including a new immersive show with Immersive Everywhere.

E.M Williams (They/Them) – Associate Director/ Movement Director

E.M is a queer, non binary theatremaker from the Midlands. Their specialisms include circus, puppetry, physicality, song and poetry, and their work in movement and performance has taken them to three continents (so far).

Rodent (They/Them) – Sound Designer

Multidisciplinary artist Rodent has been creating work for live performance and film since 2016, emerging from the underbelly of East London's drag and cabaret scenes. Combining a sonic practice with high octane spectacles of tragicomedy and monstrous camp, their work is underpinned by a fascination with the affective power of sound. Scoring and sound designing their own solo and collaborative projects, as well as for other artists and companies, Rodent is emerging as a singular voice in the worlds of sound art and performance. Rodent studied at Queen Mary University of London and credits include *Homecoming* (Fierce Festival, 2017); *Tantrum* (Steakhouse Live, 2018), Destruction/Disorder/Dirt/ Pollution (Rich Mix, 2019); *Il Widna* (dir. Joseph Wilson, 2020); *Jenny* (SPILL Festival, 2021) and *Good Clean Fun* (The Pleasance, 2022).

Martha Godfrey (They/Them) – Lighting Designer

Martha Godfrey is a lighting and projection designer based in London. Past work includes: *Bangers* (tour and Soho Theatre); *But I'm A Cheerleader* (Turbine Theatre); *Passion Fruit* (New Diorama Theatre); *Home, I'm Darling* and *Around the World in Eighty Days* (Theatre Royal Bury St Edmunds); *Oliver Twist!* (Chester Storyhouse); *What Do You See* (Shoreditch Town Hall); *Redemption* (The Big House); *Pink Lemonade* (The Bush); *Concrete Jungle Book* (The Pleasance); *Fever Pitch* (The Hope); *Time and Tide* (The Park); *Before I Was A Bear* (The Bunker); *I Wanna Be Yours* (UK tour and Bush); *Unknown Rivers* (Hampstead Downstairs); *We Dig* (Ovalhouse); *Cabildo* (Arcola Theatre); *Since U Been Gone* and *Pink Lemonade* (both Assembly Hall, Edinburgh Fringe); *Grey* (Ovalhouse); *White* (Ovalhouse, Pleasance Edinburgh Fringe, UK tour); *Exceptional Promise* (Bush); *Fuck You Pay Me* (The Bunker/Rich Mix/Assembly Rooms, Edinburgh Fringe/Vaults Festival).

Lulu Tam (She/Her) – Present-Day Costume & Set Designer

Lulu Tam is a scenographer who likes to explore materials, body, space in performance. She works nationally and internationally and her work has been shown at renowned festivals, including the Prague Quadrennial of Performance Design and Space 2011 and 2019, the London Art Biennale 2015 etc. She was a finalist for the Linbury Prize and the winner of Taking the Stage supported by British Council Ukraine in 2015. Furthermore, she was a selected designer at the World Stage Design 2017, Taipei. She is now a lecturer at the Central School of Speech and Drama.

Bethan Clark (She/Her) – Fight Director

Bethan Clark is a fight director and certified teacher with the British Academy of Dramatic Combat.

Fight direction credits include *As You Like It* (Northern Broadsides); *In Hell* (RCSSD); *The Bolds* and *Marvin's Binoculars* (The Unicorn); *Our Lady of Blundellsands* (Liverpool Everyman); *The Last Ship* (Northern Stage and US tour); *The Effect* (English Theatre Frankfurt); *Macbeth* (Queens Theatre Hornchurch and Derby Playhouse); *A View from the Bridge* (York Theatre Royal); *Our Lady of Kibeho* (Royal and Derngate, Theatre Royal Stratford East); *My Beautiful Laundrette* (Leicester Curve); *Lord of the Flies* (Theatr Clwyd and Sherman Theatre); *As You Like It* (NT Public Acts and Queens Theatre Hornchurch); *Kes* (Leeds Playhouse); *Thick as Thieves* (Clean Break and Theatr Clywyd); *The Hired Man* (Queens Theatre Hornchurch, Hull Truck and Oldham Coliseum); *Othello* (Liverpool Everyman); *Everything is Possible: The York Suffragettes* (York Theatre Royal and Pilot Theatre); *The Borrowers* (Polka Theatre); *The Picture of Dorian Gray* (Tilted Wig Productions); *In Basildon*, *Abigail's Party*, *Priscilla Queen of the Desert*, *Rope* and *The Invisible Man* (Queens Theatre Hornchurch).

Tigger Blaize (He/Him) – Intimacy Director

Tigger is originally from Guernsey, trained at Rose Bruford, and now works as an actor in theatre, TV, film and audio. As portfolio careers go, Tigger's is fairly eclectic, working as an intimacy coordinator/director, delivering workshops in Trans Awareness;

working as an LGBT+ consultant to arts organisations, ski instructing a bit in the winter, and running a monthly pavement cake shop – 'CAKE on the hEdge'.

Rebecca Cartwright (She/Her) – Historical Costume Designer & Supervisor

Rebecca started her career at the Stephen Joseph Theatre and has gone on design on several shows for Sir Alan Ayckbourn, most recently *All Lies* for The Old Laundry Theatre, whilst designing, supervising, devising and making across a broad range of performance genres and disciplines. From large scale parade puppetry (Hand Made Parade, Keep It Moving, Opera North) to political dance and performance art across Europe (Yanis Varoufakis – Democracy in Europe 2025, The International Critical Costume Symposium 2018), Rebecca has an MA in performance design from Central Saint Martins and specialises in feminist and queer devised costume performance practice. Other recent credits include mixed roles on *Notes on Grief* (Manchester International Festival); *The Ancestors* (English Heritage/National Youth Theatre); *Vanara* (Hackney Empire) and supervising on *As You Like It* (Northern Broadsides and Stoke New Vic) and *A Murder Is Announced* (Middle Ground Theatre).

ABOUT METAL RABBIT PRODUCTIONS

Metal Rabbit Productions was established in 2012, since then it has produced quality new work in London, on tour in the UK and in New York, garnering multiple OffWestEnd and Broadway World award nominations. Metal Rabbit Productions has premiered the works of Phillip Ridley and produced the debut plays by writers Lisa Carroll, John Webber, Henry Devas, Tess-Berry Hart and Mike Stone. Previous productions include *Spiderfly* (Theatre503); *We're Staying Right Here* and *Fishskin Trousers* (Park Theatre); *Cuckoo* (Soho Theatre); *Tonight With Donny Stixx* (The Bunker); *Cargo* (Arcola Theatre); *Radiant Vermin* (Bristol Tobacco Factory, Soho Theatre, 59E59 NYC); *Lardo* (Old Red Lion); *Johnny Got His Gun* (Southwark Playhouse and UK tour) and Ernest Hemingway's *Fiesta* (Trafalgar Studios).

Note From the Author

In 1988, the Conservative government passed Section 28, a law forbidding local authorities from 'promoting homosexuality.' Back then, 'homosexuality' was their catch-all term for the whole rainbow and 'promoting' meant 'mentioning' so, in addition to the silencing of teachers, LGBTQ+ books were taken off the shelves of local libraries, certain films were banned from exhibition at council venues, and some theatre groups were denied Arts Council funding for being 'too gay'. Even after the law was repealed in 2003 its long shadow created an entire generation who simply weren't told that we might be queer.

I didn't (knowingly) meet another transgender person until I was already nineteen, and when I did I lacked the education to understand them never mind realise our common nature. By then I had a whole life already in motion and a future all planned out. I had powerful reasons to stay in the closet even if it meant dying young, and that years-long mindfuck is dramatised in *The Prince*.

The text itself is a mixture of blank verse and prose. Almost all of the verse is original, with sprinklings of Bard. Writing in iambic pentameter was its own particular pleasure – the meter provided just the right constraint to inspire creativity. My favourite bits are the mail/male homonyms, the 'Was Athena the lesser for her sex?' speech, the 'Thy wit is as the sunshine' joke, and the 'Be like a lesbian' joke, all of which are said by Kate. One hazard of writing in verse however is that it can easily become too flowery: an imaginary David Mamet stood over me during bouts of editing and ripped out whole paragraphs, even whole scenes and characters, that functioned more to show off than to advance the story. Another hazard is that many theatres, I have found, do not accept new writing unless it's in prose.

The script went through many revisions, of which Version 7 is the one you hold in your hands. Version 1 was written when I was still at drama school and still in the closet; it was supposed to be about what it feels like to be a British person turning against the monarchy. It was entirely in verse and weaved in and out of *Henry IV Part 1*, inspired by Tom Stoppard's *Rosencrantz and Guildenstern Are Dead* and Tristan Bernays' *Boudica*. The end result was dense and didactic: Hotspur was visited by the three witches from *Macbeth* who turned out to be time-travelling Marxists trying to stop his wicked uncle Worcester perpetrating counterrevolution. A slog. I put it away and didn't think about it for years.

By 2020 I was out in my private life but not to the public. I went in secret to see Travis Alabanza's *Overflow* at the Bush, a play about a trans woman trapped in a toilet. I was recognised in the foyer and had to make a swift exit to avoid being outed but I came away galvanised. The isolated location of the toilet provided the protagonist an opportunity to stand outside the world and criticise it, but I wanted to write something about characters who criticised the world, as it were, from within – simultaneously immersed in and resistant to it. I returned to my text and realised it had a strong queer theme I hadn't noticed first time round: Hotspur is immersed in the closet (the world of *Henry IV*) and getting out means changing her relationships with others. I revised it to strengthen this theme and arrived at Version 2, which went out to producers and directors and began a slow roll towards the stage. I knew I was on to something when I first met my dramaturge, the wonderful Donnacadh O'Briain, and he gave me the best compliment I've ever received in my life: 'There are parts of this where I can't tell what's Shakespeare and what's you.'

By Version 3, the Marxism was gone and the queer theme was dominant. I was also playing with using prose as a way of letting characters break out of their assigned roles. I worried the play might be difficult for people who weren't already Shakespeare-heads, but then I read Paris Lees' novel *What It Feels Like For A Girl*, which uses class and location-specific vernacular to put the reader at an interpretive distance reflecting the protagonist's struggle to be correctly interpreted in their gender. It was one of the most brilliant pieces of art I had ever encountered and I was reassured that 'difficult' can be a good thing. I signed a contract with the Southwark Playhouse for a planned run in Autumn 2022 and kept writing.

In Version 4, two of the witches – Sycorax and Entjen – became Sam and Jen. I also had the mad impulse to start the second half in *Hamlet* to keep the audience on their toes. Donnacadh called it 'Elizabethan sci-fi'. I started telling friends 'It's like *The Matrix* if it was written in 1600'. Version 4 expressed my feelings well enough, but who cares? Just because you express yourself doesn't mean your art is good. The final shot of inspiration came from a musical by Chris Bush, an early draft of which I workshopped at the Donmar Warehouse. Chris's script powerfully explored trans struggles but it was also universal: the most beautiful moments came when the cis and trans characters struggled together. I realised that I needed to show not just how Hotspur was trapped, but how everyone else was too. This was the impetus behind Versions 5 and 6. Director Tash Rickman came on board. She asked me whether I had any visions for the design of the show and I said, 'Have you seen the movie *Highlander*?' Finally, after we cast the thing, Version 7 added polish, and we were ready to rehearse.

It feels strange to be putting this play on now, during a transphobic moral panic that heralds a fascist resurgence. I deliberately downplayed the queer and trans aspects in the marketing, preferring to describe it as 'a play about being trapped in bad relationships'. I didn't want to be boxed in as 'a trans writer' (I still don't); I didn't want people to overlook the arcs of the cishet characters; I wanted to avoid potential backlash; and, to be blunt, I thought we'd sell more tickets that way. Nevertheless, the heart of the show is a coming out story.

I'm often asked what I think about queer representation in the arts. On the one hand, it's nice to have and I'm pleased to have added to it. On the other, queer audiences can't pay rent with representation. As Harry Josephine Giles pointed out in their essay 'Give Up Art', to be 'an artist' (or writer or actor) is to occupy a particular position in the economy i.e. one in which you derive the majority of your income from making art. It therefore comes with bourgeois economic interests and a limited capacity to disrupt the functioning of power.

Indeed, I have some sympathy with the view that rainbow-branded art helps assuage liberals as they enable a rightward slide. Not long ago a production of *Cabaret* was mounted in London and charged around £200 a ticket – well beyond the means of most LGBT people. During the run a gay man was beaten bloody on the pavement outside in a homophobic assault perpetrated by a cisgender woman. How many of the silver haired, Range Rover owning, designer gilet-wearing audience members sitting just a few feet from that attack voted for our current government, who are presiding over a queerphobic backlash enabling such crimes and whose previous leader called gay men 'tank-topped bumboys'? How many will vote that way again because it protects their class interests, having bought their way out of guilt for the price of a ticket to *Cabaret*? That incident is no slight against the cast and crew – by all accounts the show was excellent – but it illustrates the limited power of representation. If trans people can be kicked out of our homes, denied healthcare, deadnamed and misgendered in schools or at work, discriminated against by housing authorities, shelters, sports bodies and employers, what does it matter if Abigail Thorn wrote a play? Put 'representation' in one hand and shit into the other and see which one fills up first.

And as I write these words trans people in Britain are facing a lot of shit. The NHS still forces us to use a segregated service with a 20+ year waiting list – every year at Pride we hear the names of the ones who have died waiting. We still have to apply for permission from the government's Gender Recognition Panel to get married the same way cis people do. Non-binary people are not legally recognised as existing at all. Transphobic hate crimes are soaring. Sporting agencies are banning us from competitions that we have taken part in since they began for reasons that are blatantly unsupported by evidence. Mainstream writers argue for trans children to be given conversion therapy instead of puberty blockers, a discussion rendered moot by the fact that the NHS doesn't treat them in a timely fashion anyway.

Mainstream news outlets routinely publish transphobic talking points – there is seemingly no horror that *The Guardian* will not compare us to, including climate change and Wayne Couzens. A 2021 book claiming that transness is a plot by Jewish billionaires was reviewed positively by *The Times, The Daily Telegraph, The Evening Standard, The New York Times, The New Statesman* and *The Scotsman*, none of which commented on the worrying overlap between transphobia and antisemitism.

Politicians of all parties indulge in transphobia openly: both Liz Truss and Rishi Sunak ran for Leader of the Conservative Party on explicitly transphobic platforms and multiple members of Labour's current front bench have publicly called for trans women in particular to have fewer rights than we already do. The Home Office knowingly deports LGBT people to countries where they will be killed for their sexuality or gender. The Equality and Human Rights Commission was recently caught holding secret meetings with transphobic hate groups; its head, Baroness Falkner, used her Parliamentary email account to conduct further secret correspondence and may have changed the wording of official EHRC documents at the request of those same hate groups. Former Equalities Minister Kemi Badenoch was caught sending secret letters to the Financial Conduct Authority urging them to block trans-inclusive workplace guidance policies from being issued to their member organisations. Attorney General Suella Braverman has announced that schools have no legal obligation to accommodate transgender pupils (she may in fact be legally wrong, but until someone raises the cash to test it in court her remarks may have wide-ranging effects). The government has announced it will allow conversion therapy against trans people to continue, which in practical terms means all LGBT conversion therapy will be allowed to continue – it'll simply rebrand as anti-trans.

Across the Atlantic in the USA, armed militias are disrupting Pride parades, trans children are being taken from their parents, some states are introducing their own Section 28-style laws like Florida's 'Don't Say Gay' bill, others are banning transition entirely, and there are open calls for queer people to be executed. Behind many of these horrors is the same lie that fuelled Section 28 – the lie that queerness is contagious (especially to children) and unnatural.

Once again we are the canaries in the coal mine. Cishet people, as a political class, have apparently failed to learn from their previous crimes. Grimly, it must be noted that even the most brilliant anti-fascist plays of the 1930s did nothing to prevent them sending us to the camps wearing pink triangles last time round. I cannot pretend that *The Prince* holds any solutions or that it is not part of the same system of bourgeois art. Perhaps it's a slim consolation that we received some arts council funding, which we certainly would not have done thirty years ago. All I can say is that I greatly enjoyed the process of making it and if it helps humanise queerness to you (in particular if it helps you come out) then so much the better. Whatever happens, queer people will continue to be born and we will continue to make art. Creativity, after all, entails a refusal to be eliminated from the community of human beings.

Abigail Thorn, London, Summer 2022

Acknowledgements

This play would not have come about without my agents at United – Captain Kirk, Gabi, Donovan and Caroline – and the kind people at Methuen Drama. Thank you to Paris Lees for making the introductions and being a true friend. To Alice KC, Devon, Alice QR, Niamh, Ben and Nicholas B for slogging through Version 2. To Emma Frankland for your uncompromising feedback – you were right. Thank you to Donnacadh O'Briain for seeing the potential and putting up with me calling you Donny. Thank you to Nicholas Pinnock for your encouragement and being the best mentor a young actress could wish for. To Stacy and all the girls in dolls' chat for giving me the confidence to rock a crop top on the poster. To Eleanor Janega for your historical insights. Thank you to my producers Simon and George for your rock-solid confidence and amazing powers, my director Tash Rickman, a nonpareil, and all the cast and crew of the London premiere. Thank you to Dave Wiskus – the Tony Stark of the Internet – and everyone at Standard, especially James, Nikki, PJ and Tara. Thank you especially to the fans of *Philosophy Tube* – I am in no doubt about who gave me the platform I leveraged to make this play; I'd never have made it this far without you, especially those of you who support me on Patreon. Thank you to my wonderful girlfriend – someday we will rule the world together, my love.

Lastly I'd like to thank my Mum and Dad, to whom this text is dedicated. I hope it explains a few things.

The Prince

For M&D

Casting

Hotspur, **Jen**, *and* **Sam** *must always be played by trans women. The play should never be performed by an all-white cast.*

Characters

Hotspur, *a trans woman so deep in the closet she doesn't even know it yet. The eldest child of the Earl of* **Northumberland** *and a renowned fighter. Hot-tempered, dealing with a lot of internalised misogyny and unspoken pain, has a deeply buried sweet side.*

Jen, *a baby tran from the modern day. Curious, open-hearted, compassionate.*

Sam, *a trans woman from the modern day. Highly strung, nervous, motherly.*

Lady Kate, *a woman ahead of her time.* **Hotspur***'s wife. Intelligent, determined, sexually confident.*

Prince Hal, *a gay man out to himself – it's an open secret to everyone else. The son of* **King Henry IV** *and heir to the throne. Compassionate and clever, not a fighter.*

Northumberland, *a mighty warrior in his day, now reaching his twilight years and looking to secure his legacy. Father to* **Hotspur**. *Loving and proud.*

Doubles with
King Henry IV, *an old lion backed into a corner. King of England and father of* **Prince Hal**. *Wrathful, does not accept his son's homosexuality. Quick to anger, not a great listener.*

Worcester, *a powerful noble in his own right. The younger brother of* **Northumberland**, *and uncle to* **Hotspur**. *Wise, level-headed, practical.*

Douglas, *warlord leader of the Scottish rebels. Macho and loving it. A bit of a meathead, but charming and witty when he wants to be.*

Act I

Scene I

London, Eltham Palace

Enter **King Henry**, **Jen** *and* **Sam**.

King Henry IV
So shaken as we are, so wan with care,
Find we a time for frighted peace to pant,
And breathe short-winded accents of new broils
To be commenced in strands afar remote.
No more the thirsty entrance of this soil
Shall daub her lips with her own children's blood;
Nor more shall trenching war channel her fields,
Nor bruise her flowerets with the armèd hoofs
Of hostile paces: those opposèd eyes,
Which, like the meteors of a troubled heaven,
All of one nature, of one substance bred,
Did lately meet in the intestine shock
And furious close of civil butchery
Shall now, in mutual well-beseeming ranks,
March all one way and be no more opposed
Against acquaintance, kindred and allies.
The edge of war, like an ill-sheathèd knife,
No more shall cut his master. Therefore, friends,
As far as to the sepulchre of Christ,
Forthwith a power of English shall we levy;
Whose arms were moulded in their mothers' womb
To chase these pagans in those holy fields.
But this our purpose now is twelve month old,
And bootless 'tis to tell you we will go:
Therefore we meet not now. Then let me hear
Of you, my noble lord and loyal friend,
What yesternight our council did decree
In forwarding this dear expedience.

Sam

My liege, this haste was hot in question,
And many limits of the charge set down
But yesternight: when all athwart there came
A post from Scotland, leaden with grave news.

Music. As **Sam** *outlines the following, enter* **Hotspur** *pursuing the Earl of* **Douglas** *– we are to understand that this is the battle* **Sam** *is relating, taking place not in the same location as the description but made visible for the audience's benefit.*

Sam

On Holy-rood day, the gallant Hotspur there,
Harry Percy, and the Earl of Douglas,
That ever-valiant and approvèd Scot,
At Holmedon met!

Hotspur *and* **Douglas** *fight.*

Douglas

Lay on! Lay on ya wee and scrawny thing,
I've fought grandmothers with more strength than ye!

They fight some more.

Sam

Those two did spend a sad and bloody hour,
Ten thousand bold Scots, two and twenty knights,
Balk'd in their own blood did our rider see
On Holmedon's plains. If Harry Hotspur wins,
It would be conquest for a prince to boast of.

King Henry IV

Yea, there thou makest me sad and makest me sin
In envy that my Lord Northumberland
Should be the father to so blest a son,
A son who is the theme of honour's tongue.

Hotspur *beats* **Douglas** *into retreating offstage.*

Enter an out of breath and out of his depth **Prince Hal**, *who stops to pant.*

King Henry IV
Whilst I, by looking on the praise of him,
See riot and dishonour stain the brow
Of my young Harry.

Hotspur
On your feet, Prince Hal.
These wars make men of us. Are you a man?

Prince Hal
A spent one! O, I cannot match thy pace,
My lungs will burst! Would I had never come
From cosy London to this damnèd place!

Hotspur
Then get thee to thy tent, I say, go to!
We have no use for women on the field!

Hotspur *exits.*

King Henry IV
O that it could be proved
That some night-tripping fairy had exchanged
Northumberland's child with mine when they were born,
Then would I have his Harry, and he mine.

Prince Hal *gathers himself and trundles off.*

King Henry IV
It seems then that the tidings of this broil
Brake off our business for the Holy Land
And for this cause awhile we must neglect
Our sacred purpose to Jerusalem.
Bring any word, my noble friends, you hear
Of how the battle at our border stands.
With Hotspur at its head I do not doubt
That soon we shall have victory and peace.

Jen *and* **Sam** *either bow or snap to attention as* **King Henry** *exits.*

Scene II

Continuous

Beat.

Beat.

They look to see that **King Henry** *is really gone.*

Jen (*on the edge of panic*)
  I didn't understand a bloody word of that!
  What's going on?!

Sam
  Hey, it's okay, it's okay you're all right!

Jen
  What is this?! Who was that?! Who are you?!

Sam
  Take a deep breath, you're safe, it's okay! I'm a friend!
  Here, have some water.

Sam *gives* **Jen** *a bottle of Diet Coke that has been filled with water.*
Jen *drinks and breathes.*

Sam
  I'm going to need you to remain calm, take a deep breath
  – think very carefully and calmly and can you tell me,
  what is your name?

Jen
  I'm . . . Portia. I'm Portia. I'm Brutus' wife, I have to . . .

Suddenly falling into it, speaking to nobody.

  You've ungently, Brutus,
  Stole from my bed: and yesternight, at supper,
  You suddenly arose, and walk'd about,
  Musing and sighing, with your arms across
  And when I ask'd you what the matter was –

Sam
  No no no stay with me, stay with me!

Jen

   I grant I am a woman; but withal
   A woman that Lord Brutus took to wife:
   I grant I am a woman; but withal
   A woman well-reputed, Cato's daughter –

Sam

   Snap out of it!

Jen *snaps out of it.*

Jen

   Hey! Where am I, who are you?!

Sam

   You were gone for a second there! Don't worry, it takes a
   moment to shake it off; just stay calm and think very
   carefully and clearly. Can you tell me your name?

Jen

   . . . Portia? I'm Brutus' wife.

Sam

   Are you sure it's Portia? Are you sure you're married to
   Brutus, as in Ancient Roman Brutus, best mates with
   Julius Caesar Brutus?

Jen

   Yes. I'm Portia. I'm Brutus' wife.

Sam

   What kind of bottle is that?

Jen

   Diet Coke.

Sam

   Right, now if you're from Ancient Rome how do you
   recognise Diet Coke?

Beat.

Jen

   Oh my god what the *fuck?!*

Sam

It's okay, it's okay!

Jen

Fuck, fuck, fuck! Uh . . . uh! . . .Jen, Jen, my name is Jen!
God, I completely believed I was an Ancient Roman!

Sam

That's right. I rescued you.

Sam *shakes* **Jen***'s hand vigorously.*

I'm Sam. Or Sammy or Samantha whichever you prefer.
I'm from Liverpool and I'm a manager in a care home,
which is all arse holes and noses: wiping arse holes and
wiping noses all day! But don't worry, I've washed my
hand since then! Hahahahaha!

Jen

Where am I?

Sam

Right now we're somewhere between 'in the shit' and 'in
harm's way.' Just keep your head down and do what I tell
you. Now come on – that was Scene One; it's about to
change!

Jen

Change? Into what?

Sam

Northumberland, 1402 – The Battle of Holmedon Hill!

Scene III

The Battle of Holmedon Hill

Drums sound as **Sam** *pulls* **Jen** *off and* **Hotspur** *and* **Worcester**
enter. **Worcester** *has his sword drawn. They are a little on edge –
this is a battlefield and there could be danger on all sides.* **Hotspur**
is checking the ground. The drums stop.

Hotspur
God's wounds, I thought my sword fell hereabout!

They look about for **Hotspur**'s *sword for a second.*

Worcester
Good nephew, in this battle smoke and marsh
I fear to find it is impossible!

Hotspur
I had it of my father years ago!

Worcester
That wayward blade hath done our noble cause
Great service, there's comfort: the Thane of Fife
Is taken as our prisoner, and Menteith.
I dare believe we may have victory!

Hotspur
The Earl of Douglas yet evades our grasp:
I clashed with him but dealt no fatal wound.
He slipped by me when last our armies met
At Otterburn, and left my brother dead.
I'll say when I have paid him back in blood
That we have victory, and not before.

A distant trumpet sounds from offstage.

Worcester (*pointing offstage*)
Nephew, our knights returning from their charge!
The Scottish lines are broken; we have won!

Hotspur
Yet where is Douglas?

Worcester
I cannot make him out.
But here's a friendly face!

Enter **Northumberland**.

Northumberland
My boy, my boy!

Hotspur
>   Father!

Northumberland *looks as if he is going to embrace* **Hotspur** *but then transitions into a back pat or a firm handshake.*

>   How stands the day?

Northumberland
>   My boy, the day is ours:
>   Watching from my horse I saw thee fight,
>   All glinting in the sun like mailèd Mars
>   Thy voice like thunder shook the startled birds
>   From every tree! The rabbits hereabout
>   Did dive into their burrows as in fear
>   That they beheld a second Hercules!
>   A knight who rode beside me did exclaim
>   The courage of, 'That warrior who strides
>   Into a battle like the foaming sea
>   And parts it with defiant manly will!'
>   I, swelling in my chest, with laughter turned
>   And proudly cried to all, 'He is my son!'

Worcester (*with more back patting*)
>   Thou hast brought honour to our family name!

Hotspur
>   Enough! These gilded garments fit me not,
>   What of the Earl of Douglas? Where is he?

The Earl of **Douglas** *enters, unarmed, escorted by two guards – * **Sam** *pretending and* **Jen** *pretending but still visibly confused.* **Sam** *might signal to* **Jen** *where to stand.*

Hotspur
>   Accursèd Scot! Thou savage! Thou base thing!

Douglas
>   Good morrow Harry Percy. And my lord –?

Worcester
I am Sir Thomas Percy, Earl of Worcester,
The brother of the elder Henry here.

Douglas
I see the landscape of Northumberland
Makes Percys grow like dandelions: weeds
That are cut down and then sprout up again.

Hotspur
You cut my brother Ralph down.

Douglas
Aye, I did,
When you were but a stripling, years ago.
And now I am your prisoner.

Hotspur
Not for long.
Father, lend me your sword.

Northumberland *gives* **Hotspur** *his sword.* **Douglas** *kneels.*

Douglas
Come, make it quick.
Send me to meet my cousin Archibald
Who you dispatched today, and we'll make hell
Hold three prime places for the Percy boys!

Hotspur *raises the sword to execute* **Douglas**, *but a trumpet sounds and* **Prince Hal** *enters. He has some letters with him. The Percys bow, followed by* **Sam** *and then* **Jen**, *catching up.*

Prince Hal
Make way there! In Prince Henry's name make way!
Which of you untaught knaves, unmannerly
To top the basest varlet, ranks enough
Among what out of London generously
Are flattered with the name of gentlemen
To parlay with the issue of a King?

Worcester
> These untaught knaves, my prince, have won the day
> And at a Kingly cost vanquished the Scot!

Hotspur
> Or were about to.

Prince Hal
> Nay, put up that sword!
> Deliver straight to me all Scottish prisoners
> As you may have without ransom or delay.
> I shall escort them South with every speed
> To give them up unto my father's court.

Douglas
> It seems I am reprieved.

Hotspur
> Not him: he's mine.

Prince Hal
> Read you this letter that a messenger
> Placed in my hand just moments hence! The King,
> My father, gave this urgent task to me,
> Charging that I instruct Northumberland.

Northumberland *takes the letter and reads it.*

Hotspur
> The Scots surrendered not unto the King
> But me! This is my field of victory!

Douglas
> Can I surrender for a second time?

Prince Hal
> I do accept.

Hotspur
> No! He has no command!

Prince Hal

I have command by this crown that I wear,
And by the blood I carry in my veins!

Hotspur

You have no knights on this field, no army,
You are no soldier, have not stained your sword –

Prince Hal

I marched from London to be here with you,
To oversee your lumpen, awkward war,
Braved villainous clouds of salt-petre and soot
Made blacker by egregious soldiers' oaths
And pricking marshland flies which steal my blood
By pints and gallons!

Hotspur

No, my precious prince,
You did not march here, rather were you dragged
With lumpen awkward feet and dainty hands,
Sweet breath and neatly polished fingernails,
To sit in womanly idleness on your arse!

Prince Hal

Then as the solider here, you surely know
A soldier's duty is obedience!
And my duty shall I discharge at once
In taking of your prisoners.

Hotspur

One word more
And I shall count you with my prisoners!
Your tongue advances hotly on the ground
Of soldiery and duties, yet your brain
Hath neither powers nor the discipline
Of military theoric you would need
To hold it! And your limbs would likely fail,
Unschooled, untrained as they are with a blade
Save for your pocketknife gainst Sunday beef!

Prince Hal

> This girlish tempest temper quite exceeds
> Your savage reputation.

Hotspur

> Girlish?

Prince Hal

> Ay.

Hotspur *goes for* **Prince Hal** *but* **Worcester** *gets between them and holds* **Hotspur** *back.* **Hotspur** *struggles with* **Worcester**.

Worcester

> Good nephew, cool the fire of your rage!
> Have we not spoken many times of calm
> And all the virtues that it brings a man?

Prince Hal *throws down his glove.*

Prince Hal

> There is my gage! Your hand would be advised
> To sooner touch a venomous viper's tail
> Than such a certain seal of vengeful death.
> I am, you cur, an Ares i'the field,
> You an Hephaestus, brutish and deformed!
> I'faith were there some honour in this smoke,
> These most unsporting cannons and vile guns
> That strike a good tall fellow from his horse
> Ere strength or skill at arms can be observed,
> I would myself have ta'en to soldiering
> And rivalled Alexander with a sword.

Worcester *successfully calms* **Hotspur**.

Worcester (*to* **Hal**)

> My prince, take up your gage: enough have died,
> We need not have more bloodshed. Come, let's talk.

Worcester *takes* **Prince Hal** *aside to talk to him.* **Hotspur** *speaks in an aside to the audience.*

Hotspur
Why 'girlish'? Wherefore 'girlish' sticks in me?
I am a man, no girl, that's certain! Bah!

Hotspur *thinks alone.* **Jen** *and* **Sam** *talk, unheard by the rest.*

Jen
This is fucking coconuts!

Sam
Sh!

Hotspur *goes to join* **Northumberland***.*

Northumberland
The orders from the King are genuine.
Specifically the Earl of Douglas' name
Is set down to be made a prisoner
And not the instrument of our revenge.

There's worse news in the second letter here.
Thy brother in law, that's Edmund Mortimer,
Against the irregular and wild Glendower,
Was by the rude hands of that Welshman captured.

Hotspur
Alas, that we should weigh our victory
In equal measure with such dark defeat,
That celebration lights up all the North
While funeral darkness shades the sullen South.
Then both my brothers now are lost to me;
Will neither be avenged?

Northumberland
Do not despair.
Our Ralph is gone, and taking our revenge
Could never bid him walk out of his grave.
I miss him every day. But I have found
In time the wound of grief becomes a scar,
No longer bleeding but an old complaint.
I have one son still breathing, and thy face

Alive and smiling is more dear to me
Than one more corpse left out to feed the crows.

Prince Hal *sees this tender moment between* **Northumberland**
and **Hotspur**.

Northumberland
And as for Edmund Mortimer – he lives!
So as he lives we work to set him free.
I council that we keep our prisoner
Until King Henry is of such a mind
To ransom home our cousin who is lost.

Hotspur
I am content. We shall exchange the Scot.

They turn back to **Worcester** *and* **Hal** *and now we pick up their
conversation.*

Worcester
Unless you'd name Goliath as your second
The danger doth outweigh your pride, my prince:
You have yourself seen my nephew think not
Of gralloching[1] a Scotsman in a stroke
Or mangling a Welshman so entire
That Welsh alone has words savage enough
To sound description in an English ear.

Prince Hal
I am familiar with your nephew's wrath;
How deep the currents of passion run in him.

Northumberland
Your royal highness, we propose a trade:
We'll gladly give you Douglas and the rest
If your father the King can make a vow
That he will ransom Edmund Mortimer,
Our cousin taken by the Welsh army.

---

[1] Delightful Scottish verb meaning 'to disembowel' – usually applied to deer. Involves
making a deep cut up the middle and letting the blood and organs drain out into a pit.
Worcester is speaking colourfully.

Prince Hal
    I cannot promise on the King's behalf.
    And yet I can on my own name, aye! Yes!
    This seems a friendly, even-handed suit;
    I grant it, or I shall – yes, it is done!

Douglas
    I like it!

Hotspur
    Silence, cur! Thou keep'st thy head
    But temporarily.

Douglas
    So do we all.

Worcester
    Then I suggest we draw up the details
    Not in the frigid air but in my tent,
    Where we can all repose and ease ourselves.

Taking **Hotspur** *aside*.

    Good nephew, we shall parlay with the prince,
    Find you some other task or rest alone:
    When we have reached a compact we will call.

Hotspur *nods*. **Worcester** *gives her a shoulder pat or a clap on the
arm or similar*.

Worcester
    Well fought today. Our practice has borne fruit:
    Thy swordsmanship is markedly improved.

Hotspur
    I thank thee uncle. The wounded cry for aid;
    I'll see them cared for, and retrieve my sword.
    Make sure that Douglas is kept under guard.

Douglas
    I'll rest me in the warm tent for a spell.

Everybody but **Hotspur** *goes to leave.* **Hotspur** *calls out to* **Hal** *to taunt him.*

Hotspur
My Prince! In careless passion and faint breath
From many miles of marching have you let
Your glove slip negligently from your hand.

Hal *retrieves his glove.*

Prince Hal
I would we could be friends again, Harry.
This long campaign has been a taxing road
Too often paved with bitter tears and loss,
And yet I am glad I came, for I met thee.

Hotspur *says nothing.*

Hal *leads the others out – but as they go* **Hotspur** *calls out to* **Jen**.

Hotspur
Thou, soldier! Help me find my missing sword.

Some silent and frantic gestures between **Sam** *and* **Jen** *as one is led away and the other has to remain, leaving* **Jen** *and* **Hotspur** *alone.*

Hotspur
When I pursued the Douglas as he fled
I slipped into a bog and dropped my blade.
I think it landed somewhere hereabout,
I'll search this way, and thou the other, so
We'll meet back in the middle.

Beat.

Jen (*trying to be 'Shakespearean'*)
Verily!

Beat.

They search around the edge of the space for the missing sword. After a moment, **Jen** *calls out.*

Jen

So . . . we're looking for a missing sword? Is it special? Or just – generic sword-shaped?

Hotspur

What say'st thou? Hast thou found the blasted thing?

Jen

Uh, no, still looking! (*Half to herself.*) Hate for you to lose something like that. Probably got lots of beheadings to do with it.

Hotspur

My father gave it as a gift to me.
It was to mark the day I came of age,
The day that I became a man.

Jen *looks over, noticing that something was different about this last remark. Turning back, she finds the sword.*

Jen

Found it! Here you go!

Hotspur

I felt not quite myself without it here.

Hotspur *takes it.*

The old familiar heft, the swing, the slice!
I thank thee, soldier! I am much relieved.

Jen

No worries, babe! I mean, uh . . .

I sayeth verily that there are . . . no worries, my lord!

Hotspur

Where art thou from? Thou hast a strange dialect.

Jen

I am from . . . Framlingham. I was staying here, uh, with a friend. Yeah, just down the road. That's why I'm here, I mean on, on the battlefield. I saw the battle was happening so I popped out to have a shufty, and then you won, we won, so . . . no worries!

Beat.

Hotspur
Wherever thou art from, I thank thee friend.

Hotspur *goes to leave, but –*

Jen
Can I ask a question?

Why do you talk like that?

Hotspur *apparently doesn't understand, so* **Jen** *demonstrates:*

('*Shakespearean*') Each syllable and word considerèd,
All very grand, all very much controlled,
Oh, 'thee' and 'thou' and so on and so forth.

Hotspur
I speak but as I think. My passions are
All regimented, so my thoughts, my words –

Jen
Do you speak that way because it's genuinely how you think, or do you think that way because it's how you were taught to speak?

Hotspur
I . . . (*Struggling to not speak in verse.*) I've always spoken this way: it is hard . . . It's difficult to not . . . do that.

They share a bit of a laugh.

In Framlingham, they do not talk like this
But let their thoughts spill out undisciplined?

Jen
Yeah, I mean . . . I guess.

Hotspur
Hm.
I thank thee, soldier. Go and get some rest.

Jen
   Nice to meet you.

Jen *puts out her hand to shake* **Hotspur**'s. *Just as they are about to touch* **Sam** *re-enters. As they touch – thunder, wind, smoke, coloured lights, electrical noises, incredible synthesiser drones! They grip each other's hands and* **Hotspur** *is brought to her knees. They are both shocked by a powerful magical force that seems to pass between them like a current.*

The house lights briefly flash up, illuminating the audience, and then down again. They let go and fall back. **Sam** *rushes forward to help* **Jen** *offstage and they exit leaving* **Hotspur** *on the floor. The force disperses and things return to normal.*

The scene changes to –

Scene IV

Alnwick Castle Grounds

Enter **Lady Kate***, who sees* **Hotspur** *on the ground.*

Lady Kate
   My husband, are you hurt? My, what a fall!

Hotspur
   I fell?

Lady Kate
   I fear thou hit thy head; come, let me see.
   There is no blood. Nay, do not try to stand
   But rest a moment. Let me see thy arm.
   Can'st bend it? Good, it is not broken then.

Hotspur
   I'm not sure what just happened.

Lady Kate
   Thou wert recounting the exciting tale
   Of battling Douglas up at Holmedon Hill;

Thou leapt up on the wall to demonstrate
Some action and thy footing must have slipped!

Suppressing a laugh.

Thou foolish thing! We are most fortunate
Thou did'st not land upon thy sword, my love!

Hotspur (*disoriented*)
My sword? This? Is this my sword? And this, this that I'm
wearing, is this my armour?

Lady Kate
All handsomely in mail you are arranged.

Hotspur
Was there a woman here a second ago? I swear I was just
chatting with someone . . .

Lady Kate
I am the only woman here my love.

Hotspur *looks in her eyes and seems to get her groove back.*

Hotspur
Of course. Of course, my Kate. I'll try to keep
My feet on firmer ground from now on, eh?

They stand. Perhaps they dust **Hotspur** *off together.*

Lady Kate
Thou wert just telling me of Edmund then?

Hotspur
Yes, Edmund! We have asked the Prince of Wales
To intervene at court with his father,
Persuading King Henry to ransom him.
I know the Earl of Douglas vexes thee –

Lady Kate
Aye, some! Thou let him stay in this, our home!

Hotspur
It is a temporary lodging, love.

With temporary longing shall I leave
Thee soon to find a double remedy
For both thy woes – exchanging our Edmund
For that same Scot.

Enter **Northumberland**.

Northumberland
Your horse is saddled and we stay for you.
Good morrow Kate.

Lady Kate (*curtseying*)
Good morrow, noble father.

Hotspur
I must away to London. Farewell love!
I thought there was another woman here.
How odd. I would be mad if e'er I wished
To have another woman's company
When thou art fairest of the fairer sex.

Lady Kate
Oh Harry, what a flatterer thou art!
Thy tongue produces surfeit of sweet words.

Hotspur (*just to her*)
What other task then shall I set it to?
What still more pleasing service can my tongue
Perform, my Lady Kate?

Lady Kate (*playfully*)
Thou naughty man!
My innocent ears should not hear such things, sir!
Thy wit is like the sunshine: though it warms,
In tarrying in't I fear I shall turn pink!

Hotspur
A pretty jest! Thy lips have talent too.
If my tongue and thy lips worked hand in hand;
What splendid poetry they could devise.

Not wanting to third-wheel, **Northumberland** *exits.* **Kate** *notices when he goes and turns up the heat.*

Lady Kate
   My lips and thy tongue, sayest thou? And what else?

Kate *suggestively grabs the pommel of* **Hotspur**'s *sword and* **Hotspur** *pulls away sharply, smiling but a little uncomfortable.*

Hotspur
   It is a pity I must ride away.

Lady Kate
   I'd rather I than thy horse under thee!

Hotspur
   Peace, love! Wouldst lay me down on muddy grass?

Lady Kate
   The grass would be the luckiest in the world
   If thou wouldst only be on top of it!
   But I could spare thee from the mud and lie
   Between thee and the grass, if thou did wish!

Hotspur *smiles but does not reciprocate.*

Lady Kate
   Then go thou with my love.

They hold each other.

   I loathe these days,
   Too frequent and too hastily announced,
   When we must part, thou out into the world
   And I for Alnwick Castle's lonely spires.

Hotspur
   It is my duty.

Lady Kate
   Am I thy duty?

Hotspur
   Aye.

Beat – **Kate** *was hoping to be seen as a bit more than a duty!*

> My joy. The better half of all my life.
> What would a husband be without his wife?

They kiss and exit separately.

Scene V

Continuous

Sam *enters cautiously, checking* **Hotspur** *and* **Kate** *are gone. Satisfied, she doubles back and brings* **Jen** *on, supporting her.*

Jen
> Ow! Ow!

Sam
> Poor sausage, poor old thing! That's all right!

Jen
> My whole arm's got pins and needles.

Sam
> That's all right, don't you worry, Sammy's here. Can you wiggle your fingers? Good, I don't think anything's too badly hurt.

Jen
> Felt like sticking a fork in a plug socket!

Sam
> Silly old sausage!

Jen
> What is going on here?

Sam
> All right. This might be a lot to process my lovely but . . . you're inside a play.

Beat.

Jen
> What the *fuck?!*

Sam

Actually, it's a whole dimension of plays, a whole multiverse! I don't know whether we're lying in a coma up there or if we're sharing the same dream, but . . . Last thing I remember from the real world I was dropping off to sleep in the back of my car and the next thing I knew I was Cleopatra, ruling over Ancient Egypt! Which had its perks, but it all seemed a bit *weird*. And I still had my bag with me so when I saw the Diet Coke bottle I thought, 'That's funny – they don't have Diet Coke in Ancient Egypt.' And that's when it hit me, it wasn't just Ancient Egypt, it was *Antony and Cleopatra,* as in the play *Antony and Cleopatra,* as in . . . Shakespeare!

Beat.

Jen

Oh bloody hell, I hate Shakespeare.

Sam

I did a runner, wound up in *The Tempest* then *A Midsummer Night's Dream* and a bunch more, went through all the Roman ones – saw you in *Julius Caesar* and my first thought was 'Gosh, I've got to get her out of here because she's . . . you know . . . like me.'

Actually, my first thought was 'Gosh, isn't she gorgeous, hahahaha!' I imagined that you had a very glamorous lifestyle somewhere with lots of friends and a gazillion Instagram followers who'd all be missing you!

I'm nattering! Sorry!

It's just been such a long time since I've had anyone to really talk to!

Jen

That's all right – at least I can understand what you're saying!

We're inside Shakespeare?

Sam
Yes.

The play, not the man.

Jen (*taking her phone out*)
Right, I'm calling 999.

Sam
It's dead.

Jen*'s phone is indeed dead.*

Jen
Have you got a charger?

Sam
I've got something better!

Sam *produces a magic map.*

Ta-dah! I picked this up when I was down in *The Tempest*; nicked it right out from under old Prospero's nose. It's got everything on it – like magical Google.

Jen
What is it?

Sam
A map!
Although I did steal it from a wizard, darling; it's not exactly Ordnance Survey.

Sam *grandly reveals the true extent of the magic map.*

Jen
Wow . . .

Sam
Mmm. Trippy. All the different plays – they're all separated into their own little worlds. And these are the doorways between them. All you have to do is be in the right place at the right time and you can jump through.

We hear snippets of Shakespeare floating through.

Jen

Why do they talk like that?

Sam

They have a rhythm. Iambic pentameter.

Jen

I-amb what?

Sam

Verse!

Sam *and* **Jen** *put their hands on the map and* **Sam** *taps it delicately.*

Sam

Dah-dum-de-dum-de-dum-de-dum-de-dum . . .

The map taps back, dah-dum-de-dum-de-dum-de-dum-de-dum

Jen

Oh my gosh, it's like a little heartbeat!
Which play are we in?

Sam

That's the good news! We are right at the beginning of
Henry IV Part 1! I've been trying to get here for ages! Look
at this – this big doorway right at the top, read that there,
what does it say?

Jen

'Out.'

Sam

The doorways always appear at moments of choice – forks
in the road – and at the end of this play there's a great big
one! The prince starts off a mess but he puts aside his
wayward youth. He has to *choose* between his old life and
the role he was born to play, so! If we can follow him, lurk
in the background of his scenes and stick to him like glue,
eventually we'll come across this great big beautiful
doorway and that, that Jen, is 'Out'!

Jen

Do we maybe wanna ask some of the people who are already down here about it? I spoke to that girl, the one who lost her sword –

Sam

NO!

They're . . . antibodies. Characters. Do you know what the definition of a character is? 'Something that has the *appearance* of being human.'

Down here is their home, and they like it just the way it is.

Jen

Can they hurt us?

Sam

They can do worse than that. If they sucked you into playing a role in their story again you might be stuck down here forever! That's why in future I'd appreciate it if you were a bit more 'ears open' when I'm giving you instructions.

Jen

Sorry.
But for future reference, if they speak to me what am I supposed to do?

Sam

If you have to improvise, don't break the rhythm: if they give you six beats give four back, if they give you three, give them seven. It always adds up to ten. As long as you're in rhythm they see what they want to see.

The scene starts to change.

It's changing!

Scene VI

London, Eltham Palace

Enter **King Henry**, **Worcester** *and* **Hotspur** *in mid-argument.*
Sam *and* **Jen** *pretend to be guards.*

Worcester
Those prisoners in your highness' name demanded,
Which Harry Percy here at Holmedon took,
Were, as he says, not with such strength denied
As is deliver'd to your majesty!
Either envy, therefore, or misprison
Is guilty of this fault, not him, my King.

Hotspur
My liege, I did deny no prisoners –

Loudly and chaotically enter **Prince Hal**, *late.*

King Henry IV
How like a comet comes the Prince of Wales,
Amazing all and yet so seldom seen
That all our sagely wise astronomers
Can ne'er predict his visits to our court!

Prince Hal
Good gentlemen, I beg your patience,
I was detained upon an urgent . . . thing.

Hotspur (**Henry** *silences* **Prince Hal** *and bids* **Hotspur** *continue.*)
My liege, I did deny no prisoners,
But I remember, when the fight was done,
When I was dry with rage and extreme toil,
Breathless and faint, leaning upon my sword,
Came there . . . a certain lord, neat, and trimly dress'd,
Fresh as a bridegroom; and his chin new reap'd
Show'd like a stubble-land at harvest-home.
And as the soldiers bore dead bodies by,
He call'd them untaught knaves, unmannerly!
With many holiday and lady terms
He question'd me; amongst the rest, demanded

My prisoners in your majesty's behalf.
I then, all smarting with my wounds being cold,
Out of my grief and my impatience,
Answer'd neglectingly I know not what,
He should or he should not; for he made me mad
To see him shine so brisk and smell so sweet
And talk so like a waiting-gentlewoman
Of guns and drums and wounds – God save the mark!
This bald unjointed chat of his, my lord,
Was answer'd indirectly, as I said.

King Henry IV
This lord who so provoked your heated words,
What was his name?

Beat as **Hotspur** *meets* **Prince Hal***'s eyes.*

Hotspur
I cannot recall, my liege.

Pause.

Something is wrong. **Sam** *gestures to* **Jen***.*

Jen
Oh!

Consulting the map.

The circumstance consider'd, good my lord,
Whate'er Lord Harry Percy then had said
May reasonably die and never rise
To do him wrong or any way impeach
What then he said, so he unsay it now.

Worcester
Well said, my noble knight.

King Henry IV
Why, yet he doth deny his prisoners,
But with proviso and exception,
That we at our own charge shall ransom straight
His brother-in-law, the foolish Mortimer;

Who, on my soul, hath wilfully betray'd
The lives of those that he did lead to fight
Against that great magician, damn'd Glendower.
Shall we buy treason? And indent with fears,
When they have lost and forfeited themselves?
No, on the barren mountains let him starve;
For I shall never hold that man my friend
Whose tongue shall ask me for one penny cost
To ransom home revolted Mortimer.

Hotspur

Revolted Mortimer!
He never did fall off, my sovereign liege,
But by the chance of war!

King Henry IV

Thou dost belie him, Percy, thou dost belie him;
Art thou not ashamed? But, sirrah, henceforth
Let me not hear you speak of Mortimer.
Send me your prisoners with the speediest means,
Or you shall hear in such a kind from me
As will displease you. Look to it at once!

King Henry *exits.* **Jen** *moves slightly as if to go too but* **Sam**
silently gestures not yet.

Prince Hal

Good Harry Percy, might I have a word?

Worcester *gives them some space.*

I thank thee that thou chose to overlook
My name when thou recounted Holmedon's fray;
I must express my earnest gratitude.

Hal *tries to hug* **Hotspur** *but is rebuffed.*

Hotspur

Your gratitude is worth nothing to me
Whilst Mortimer my brother lies in chains
And we men of the North who won that crown
That your father so proudly wears are dogged
At every turn by his misgovernance!

Prince Hal
Let not his wrathful mood affright your heart;
I am the cause of his distemperment.

With tender difficulty.

He sees that I am yet to take a wife
And worries I am not the marriage type.

He loves thee well, and heartily desires
That I reform myself to be like thee.

Therefore, if it should please thee, stay at court
And join me in a hunt, or else at dice,
Or tennis. Therein serve a double aim:
Convince my father that I spend my time
In company of which he doth approve
And by that feint we calm his stormy mood –
Thy suit for Mortimer may yet succeed!

And secondly we serve our private aim.
Which is, if I have read thy heart correct –

Hotspur
Is this the business that the Prince of Wales
Finds suits his majesty, eh? Tennis? Dice?
Are't so effeminate? Are't so attuned
To that degenerate company you keep?
Whose prince is this, who minces and who chats
More like a Princess than a royal heir?

Beat. **Hal** *is hurt.*

Prince Hal
I know you love your brother Mortimer,
And for that love, and that which I bear you,
I shall attempt to calm my father's storm.
Meantime, my lords, obedience is due;
Send us your prisoners, or you will hear of it.

Exit **Prince Hal**. **Sam** *gives the nod to* **Jen** *and they start to slip out quietly underneath the following.*

Hotspur
> An' if the devil come and roar for them,
> I will not send them: I will after straight
> And tell him so; for I will ease my heart,
> Albeit I make a hazard of my head!

Worcester
> What, drunk with choler? Stay and pause awhile.
> Remember calm, remember reason, think!

Worcester *paces aside to cudgel his brain.* **Hotspur** *flags down* **Jen**.

Hotspur
> Soldier! The old Earl of Northumberland
> Is waiting just outside; he was dismissed
> In rage by King Henry. Go fetch him in.

Sam
> We shall obey at once, my lord Hotspur.

Hotspur (*to* **Jen**)
> Have we met?

Sam (*jumping in*)
> Yes, quite possibly, perhaps:
> We have been guarding this palace for years,
> Your lordship might have seen us here before.

Hotspur
> What is thy name, soldier?

Jen (*counting syllables on her fingers behind her back*)
> Why . . . Jen, my lord.

Hotspur
> Come, shake my hand.

Jen
> Thy hand, my lord? What for?

Hotspur
> In friendship or in enmity, choose one;
> I care not, simply do as thou art told –
> Give me thy hand.

Jen

Okay. Yes. Here it is.

Jen *holds out her hand. She and* **Sam** *brace for another explosive reaction like in Scene III, but this time it's just a normal handshake.*

Hotspur

I thank thee.

Jen

No problem-o. We'll fetch him,
The man thou did request to see just now.
In fact I see him coming already, so,
We'll see thee later, alligato-or!

Jen *and* **Sam** *exit hurriedly.*

Northumberland *enters from behind* **Hotspur**.

Worcester

Brother, the King hath forcibly denied
Our pleas to ransom Edmund Mortimer!

Northumberland

What happened? What was said when I was gone?

Hotspur

He will forsooth have all our prisoners,
And when –

Hotspur *turns to face* **Northumberland** *(who is played by the same actor who plays* **King Henry***) and double takes.*

Worcester *carries on.*

Worcester

And when we urged the ransom once again
Of our dear cousin, then his cheek look'd pale,
And on my face he turn'd an eye of death,
Trembling even at the name of Mortimer!

Worcester *leads* **Northumberland** *away to conspire with him quietly.* **Hotspur** *speaks in an aside:*

Hotspur

Is King Henry not my father's very twin?
How is't I have never marked it once before?
They are as like as this hand to itself!
What, is God's highest so common in form
That Kings are found in twos? And all alone!
Save for those guards – that Jen, whose face I think
I have encountered once before somewhere
And Henry Prince of Wales, that libertine,
Where was King Henry's retinue, his queen,
His knights, his courtiers, his people . . . shouldn't there
be, like, more people here, or something?

To an audience member directly.

Who the fuck are you?

Worcester *and* **Northumberland** *come back to include* **Hotspur**.
Worcester's *lines degenerate into iambic gibberish: he and*
Northumberland *appear not to notice but* **Hotspur** *does.*

For the benefit of the actor, the original lines – i.e. what the
characters are trying to express – are provided beneath in italics.

Worcester

Good cousin, give me audience a while!
And now I will unclasp a secret book,
And to your bluh bluh-bluh-bluh bluh-bluh-bluh
                    And to your quick conceiving discontents
Bluh bluh bluh bluh-bluh bluh bluh bluh-bluh-bluh,
                    I'll read you matter deep and dangerous
Bluh bluh bluh bluh-bluh bluh bluh-bluh-bluh bluh
                    As full of peril and adventurous spirit
Bluh bluh bluh-bluh bluh blub-bluh bluh-bluh bluh
                    As to o'er walk a current roaring loud
Bluh bluh bluh-bluh-bluh bluh-bluh bluh bluh bluh
                    On the unsteadfast footing of a spear.

Hotspur

. . .What did you just say?

Underneath this, **Hotspur** *notices the set.*

Northumberland (*to* **Worcester**)
  De dum, de dum de, dum King dum-de dum
            But soft, I pray you; did King Richard then
  De-dum de dum-de dum-de dum-de-dum
                Proclaim our cousin Edmund Mortimer
  De dum the crown?
                        Heir to the crown?

Worcester
  Bluh bluh. Bluh-bluh bluh bluh bluh.
                    He did. Myself did hear it.

Northumberland
  De, dum de dum-de dum de dum-de King
            Nay, then I cannot blame his cousin king,
  De dum de dum de dum-de dum-de dum!
          That wished him on the barren mountains starve!

Worcester (*back to* **Hotspur**)
  Bluh bluh bluh bluh bluh bluh-bluh bluh-bluh-bluh,
          Then once more to your Scottish prisoners.
  Bluh-bluh-bluh bluh bluh –
                    Deliver them up –

Hotspur (*trying to point out the set*)
  Wait wait, look at this place – look at them, who are they?

Worcester
  Bluh bluh bluh bluh bluh-bluh bluh bluh-bluh-bluh!
              You lend no ear unto my purposes!

Northumberland *continues outlining the plan, approaching*
Hotspur. *He turns back to* **Worcester** *as he speaks, clapping a*
hand on **Hotspur**'s *shoulder. As soon as his hand makes contact*
with **Hotspur** *the world snaps back to normal and his words*
instantly become understandable again.

Northumberland
  De dum-de dum my son be so employed,
            In Scotland shall my son be so employed . . .

And then the power of Scotland and of York
To join with Mortimer in rebellion,
Bearing our fortunes in our own strong arms,
Which now we hold at much uncertainty.
In faith, it is exceedingly well aim'd.

Worcester

My lords, farewell: no further go in this
Than I by letters shall direct your course.

Northumberland

Farewell, good brother: we shall thrive, I trust.

Worcester

Brother, Adieu. O, let the hours be short
Till fields and blows and groans applaud our sport!

Worcester *shakes hands manfully with* **Northumberland** *and* **Hotspur** *and exits.* **Northumberland** *turns back to* **Hotspur** *quizzically.*

Northumberland

You broke away, my boy, you marked us not!
Why, what a wasp-stung and impatient fool
Art thou to break into this woman's mood!

Hotspur

A woman's mood? What you talking about? Do I seem
womanly to you? My moods are male!

Northumberland

My son, are you quite well?

Hotspur

I'm fine.

Northumberland

E'en now you seemed distracted by something?

Hotspur

I dunno, I thought I saw someone and then, I thought I
was . . .

Northumberland *places a hand on her shoulder again.* **Hotspur**
recovers – she can't see the audience anymore.

Hotspur
  I did attend your words, father, I did.
  Rebellion is our aim, we shall seek out
  A head of safety with the Archbishop
  Of York, and Glendower and Douglas too,
  And Mortimer, to overthrow the King.

Beat. **Northumberland** *looks concerned.* **Hotspur** *breaks away.*

Hotspur
  Why turn you these dark thunderclouds on me?

Northumberland (*trying to be soothing*)
  No thunderclouds, my son, but gentle rain.
  I see some worm work deeply in thy core,
  A secret worry disfigures thy brow
  In such a pattern I have seen before:
  T'was oft thy mother's, well do I recall
  That same expression stamped across her face.

Hotspur
  My mother looked like me?

Northumberland
  In subtle ways.
  Uncanny is the likeness in your looks
  When thou art chewing on some gristly thought.
  Hence I did say, 'This woman's mood' of thine,
  I meant not to offend thy manly heart.

Beat. Perhaps they sit, if there is somewhere to do it.

At some point under the following, **Hal** *enters unseen and listens in.*

Northumberland
  Unfold to me thy cares, my son. Yet not,
  Let me divine them from thy face!

  A-ha!
  I have it, I do smell it well, indeed.
  The Lady Kate, thy thoughts do turn to her.

Implying that she is pregnant.

> There is some roundness to her figure, no?
> Some stirrings of a precious life, begun?
> And thou art, as a father soon to be,
> All plagued with fear and doubt, and so this talk
> Of civil buffeting and open war
> Hath made thee fearful for thy progeny,
> Begetting heirs into a dangerous world!

Hotspur
> No, father. Your old eyes do play you false,
> No grandsires yet have Lady Kate and I
> Begot for you. Unless there be some news
> That she has not seen fit to tell me of.

Northumberland (*beat, then a little disappointed but trying to reassure her*)
> All things in time, my son.

Hotspur
> All things in time.

Hotspur *tries to leave, but –*

Northumberland
> But one thing more. I love thee, Harry.
> Thou art mine only son, my heir, my boy.
> Thy cares are mine, thy victories and thy pains,
> And I am proud of thee. Be sure of that.

Hotspur
> Your love I do return in kind, and more,
> I shall endeavour to the utmost reach
> To earn your pride and trust in this, our war.
> And men shall say when golden gains are won,
> A mighty father sired a worthy son!

They exit. **Hal** *watches them go.*

Scene VII

Continuous

Sam *and* **Jen** *enter and spot* **Prince Hal**, *who is thinking to himself.*

Sam
  There they go, and there he is. Good! We're on track, we'll be out of here in no time!

Jen
  I think I'm getting the hang of this place! Did you see that bit of improv, serving ten syllables back every time, just bam, bam!

Sam
  Except for when you called Hotspur 'thou' instead of 'you!' In Shakespeare, calling someone 'you' implies respect; calling someone 'thou' implies familiarity or intimacy.

Jen
  Are you having a laugh?

Sam
  What?

Jen
  Are you telling me that every two minutes these fucking cis people change their pronouns?

If the audience do not laugh here, they are wrong.

  I can't even get a passport in she/they and the bloody King of England goes 'Actually my pronouns are thee/thou'?!

Jen *makes a noise of frustration, but recovers quickly.*

  I can see why people like this stuff. Those two – the prince and Hotspur, oh my god, adorable, like super tragic but just . . . argh! So much drama, I love it! Does it have a happy ending?

Sam

It doesn't matter, my love so long as we find that doorway out.

Jen

Right, right. . . . But does it have a happy ending though?

Sam

Let's stay in the now. If we're where I think we are Prince Hal's about to have a massive row with his Dad.

Jen

What? Oh no!

Enter **King Henry**.

King Henry IV

Lords, give us leave; the Prince of Wales and I
Must have some private conference; but be near at hand,
For we shall presently have need of you.

Jen (*clearly making it up on the fly, counting syllables behind her back again*)

Yet wait, my sovereign king! Let us not go
Just yet, we can be of some use to thee – you, to you!
Don't argue with your son, he is a nice
Boy and we have heard good things about him,
That you will want to know, such as . . . Uh . . .

Sam

What are you doing?!

Jen

Trying to help! Here, look at this:

Jen *tries to take out the Diet Coke bottle and show* **Hal** *but he takes her into an aside without looking at it.*

Prince Hal

I know you'd spare me from my father's words,
And I am grateful for your efforts, friend,
But they shall only spur his anger on.
Do as he says – I can withstand his rage.

Jen
  Are you sure? This is super fucked up like what's his
  problem? You're gay – so what? Or 'not the marriage type'?

Beat.

  Like that's what it's about right? . . . It's okay! Who cares!

Beat. **Hal** *is moved by someone actually saying it.*

Prince Hal
  The Prince of Wales is all that I can be.
  Yet I appreciate thy honest tongue;
  Would honesty were all my role demanded.

Hal *holds out his hand to shake* **Jen**'s. *As they touch there is another
moment of magical connection. This time it isn't painful or shocking
like* **Hotspur**'s *was, but* **Jen**, **Hal** *and* **Sam** *see and hear it.*

King Henry *does not however, and jumps in:*

King Henry IV
  We are accustomed, when we give commands,
  To having them obeyed, and promptly! Go!
  Be at both entrances, let none come in!

King Henry *dismisses* **Jen** *and* **Sam** *to opposite edges of the space
where they face outwards like guards.*

King Henry IV
  I know not whether God will have it so,
  For some displeasing service I have done,
  That, in his secret doom, out of my blood
  He'll breed revengement and a scourge for me;
  But thou dost in thy passages of life
  Make me believe that thou art only mark'd
  For the hot vengeance and the rod of heaven
  To punish my mistreadings. Tell me else,
  Could such inordinate and low desires,
  Such barren pleasures, rude society,
  As thou art matched withal and grafted to –

Prince Hal

So please your majesty, I would I could
Quit all offences with as clear excuse –

King Henry IV

The hope and expectation of thy time
Is ruin'd, and the soul of every man
Prophetically doth forethink thy fall.

Prince Hal

Do not think so; you shall not find it so.

King Henry IV

It has been found; why shall I not believe
That which is proved? Or canst thou summon up
Some words that might excuse thy vulgar choice
To live so far from all propriety?

Hal *tries to speak, but is continually interrupted.*

What say'st thou? How canst thou account for this?
Why dost thou set thy will so contrary
To wisdom and to prudence? Why dost thou?
Indulging thy desires, deepening them,
Not reigning thyself in, as princes should?

Prince Hal

I shall hereafter, my thrice gracious lord,
Be more myself!

King Henry IV

Thyself! Hotspur hath more
Loyalty, more worthy interest to the state
Than thou the shadow of succession;
But wherefore do I tell these news to thee?
Why, Harry, do I tell thee of my foes,
Which art my near'st and dearest enemy?
Who squanders years of true paternal love,
To show how much thou art degenerate!

Hal *has no reply. Exit* **King Henry** *on* **Sam**'s *side. Beat.*

Prince Hal
  Yeah. Cool. Sick. Cheers Dad. Hotspur's a legend actually.
  Completely! Fair play!

Hal *impersonates* **Hotspur**.

Prince Hal
  He's like 'I killed a dozen Scottish people today, huh-hah!
  Huh-hah! Legend! I have a sexy wife! She's like, "Oh
  Harry, how many hast thou killed today?" and I'm like,
  "Feed my horse, bitch!" Grrrrr! Oh, I must have my
  prisoners! I must have Mortimer back King Henry – I'm a
  very serious person!'

Now impersonating his father.

  'Yes, Harry Hotspur – I take you very seriously! This is the
  most dynamite shit I have ever *seen*! Oh and by the way
  congratulations on your very sexy wife!'

(**Hotspur**)
  'Thank you! I won her in a fight I had with a wolf!'

(**King Henry IV**)
  A wife worthy of a Prince! Oh, how I wish you were my
  son, and then I would have a sexy daughter in law! I wish
  my son would obtain a sexy wife! He spends all of his time
  with men – for reasons that are *somehow. Still.* A mystery to
  me!

(**Hotspur**)
  'Oh King Henry, your son is a nancy boy! He has clean
  fingernails and he combs his hair and he does not have a
  very sexy wife! He knows nothing of the pussy! He is
  unquestionably a faggot of the most heinous disposition!
  Take me as your son instead!'

(**King Henry IV**)
  'Yes! That is absolutely a sensible reaction to my son's
  homosexuality, and not at all likely to scar him for life. I
  am an extremely good father!'

  Cheers Dad! Yeah! Yeah! NICE ONE!

Beat.

Prince Hal *gathers himself and leaves the opposite way.* **Sam** *runs to* **Jen**.

Jen
  I'm sorry!

Sam
  Sorry's not enough to be frank with you! We might really
  be in the shit here now – come on!

Sam *runs out after* **Prince Hal**, *but before* **Jen** *can make it off the scene changes to –*

Scene VIII

Alnwick Castle

Jen
  Ohhhh shit.

  Jen, you've porked it now, babes. Okay, no worries. Magic
  map, easy.

Jen *checks the map and finds where she is.*

  'Northumberland, Alnwick Castle, Several Weeks Later.'

Enter **Hotspur** *with the Earl of* **Douglas**. **Jen** *scampers somewhere out of the way where she can watch. Possibly she sits in the front row of the audience.*

Douglas
  My gracious host! I must express my thanks:
  Your hospitality has been so mild,
  Your castle such a welcoming respite
  I almost could believe we had been friends
  These last few years and not dire enemies!

Hotspur
  Indeed, it seems mere minutes since we fought
  A bloody battle up at Holmedon Hill.

Douglas
I'faith I curse myself I was not ta'en
To be your lordship's prisoner before!
In gratitude I shall commit my strength
To topple Henry Bolingbroke, your king.
With Harry Hotspur fighting on our side,
I have no doubt we shall find swift success!

Hotspur
Well said, and many thanks, my noble Scot.

Douglas *and* **Hotspur** *shake hands manfully.* **Kate** *enters.*

Douglas
Ah, Lady Katherine! My humble thanks
For all thy golden generosity!
I'm glad I saw you ere we part to say:
Truly, by'm'heart thou art so becoming
Truly, my heart breaks that I'll be-going!

Douglas *kisses* **Kate**'s *hand.*

Douglas (*To* **Hotspur**.)
We'll muster up our cousins and ride south
To join with you at Bangor by the ninth.
Thanks once again, old foe and new-forged friend.

Hotspur
I'll ride out with you till our paths diverge.

Hotspur *and* **Douglas** *try to leave.*

Lady Kate
Yet stay, my husband. We must talk.

Beat.

Douglas
Uh-oh!

Hotspur (*to* **Douglas**)
I'll join you momentarily.

Douglas
  Good luck!

Douglas *exits*.

Hotspur
  How now, my wife? Have you some suit to me?

Lady Kate
  A suit? Am I to make appointments now,
  To speak with thee? My hennin is upstairs;
  Shall I put on my formal robes, my lord?

Hotspur
  Nay, but speak quickly: I am called away.

Lady Kate
  'Tis true thou art, my husband, called 'away';
  'Away' should be thy middle name, i'faith,
  For when I call out 'Harry' these stone walls
  Repeat 'Away', 'Away', in echoing sobs.
  For what offence have I these long months been
  A banished woman from my Harry's bed?
  No tenderness have I of thee enjoyed,
  No kisses, nor no touches, comforts, sighs,
  In weeks, nay months! Unnatural spans of time!
  Some heavy business hath my lord in hand:
  In thy faint slumbers I by thee have watched;
  Thy spirit within thee hath been so at war
  That beads of sweat have stood upon thy brow
  Like bubbles in a late-disturbèd stream.
  And so I counselled myself but to wait,
  Abiding patiently with solitude
  As barren trees abide with wintry frosts
  In hope of sunlit springs. But good my lord,
  I am thy wife; aren't not my husband too?
  Am I not pleasing to thee anymore?

Hotspur (*addressing* **Jen**)
  What, ho!

Jen
  Hoe? Me?

Hotspur
  Hath Butler brought those horses from the sheriff?

Jen
  One horse, my lord, he brought it even now.

Hotspur
  Bid Butler lead him forth into the park.

Jen *sees that* **Kate** *is upset and does not exit.* **Hotspur** *gestures for her to go, and she starts to.*

Lady Kate
  But hear you, Harry.

Hotspur
  What say'st thou, my lady?

Jen *lingers at the edge of the space and watches.*

Lady Kate
  What is it carries you away?

Hotspur
  My horse!

Lady Kate
  I'll know thy business, Harry, that I will.
  I fear my brother Mortimer doth stir
  About his title, and hath sent for thee
  To line his enterprise: but if you go –

Hotspur
  So far afoot, I shall be weary, love!

Lady Kate
  I must know, Harry, else thou love'st me not!

Hotspur
  Away, away, you trifler! Love! I love thee not,
  I care not for thee, Kate: this is no world

To play with mammets and to tilt with lips:
We must have bloody noses and crack'd crowns
And pass them current too. God's me, my horse!

*This last shout was to **Jen**, who hurriedly goes to exit but then lingers again even closer to the edge of the space.*

Hotspur

What wouldst thou, Kate? What woulds't thou have
with me?

Lady Kate

Do you not love me? Do you not, indeed?

Hotspur

Come, wilt thou see me ride?
And when I am on horseback, I will swear
I love thee infinitely. But hark you, Kate;
Whither I go, nor reason whereabout:
Whither I must, I must; and, to conclude,
This evening must I leave you, gentle Kate.
I know you wise, but yet no farther wise
Than Harry Percy's wife: constant you are,
Yet constantly you are a woman, Kate,
And so far will I trust you.

Lady Kate

Oh! So far!

Hotspur

Not an inch further. But hark you, Kate:
Whither I go, thither shall you go too;
Today I will set forth, tomorrow you.
Will this content you, Kate?

Lady Kate

It must, of force.

Hotspur *tries to kiss **Kate** on the cheek but she pulls away.*

Hotspur *exits.* **Jen** *goes to leave too – she is supposed to – but she sees* **Kate** *trying to hold it together and decides to stay. She cautiously approaches* **Kate***.*

Jen
Are you all right?

Lady Kate
What sayest thou, good maid?

Jen (*counting syllables behind her back again*)
I said . . . are you . . . alright?

Lady Kate
I do not need attending at this time.

Jen
. . . Okay.

Jen *goes to leave. But then –*

Lady Kate
Art married?

Jen
Married? Me?

Lady Kate
Yes. Art thou wed?

Jen
Uh, no.

Lady Kate
Ah. Well.

Beat.

Jen
Probably have to work at it, I imagine?

Lady Kate
Yes, work! Thou art correct. It is hard work.

Jen
. . . I'm sure she loves you really.

Lady Kate
She?

Jen (*correcting herself*)
He, him,
Your . . . husband, Hotspur. I'm sure he loves you really.

Lady Kate
Sometimes I feel I do not know the man:
I gaze rather upon a fixed portrait,
A hollow suit of armour brought to life.

Jen
Yeah . . . You know what uh, what men are like!

Lady Kate
Has't thou experience with men? With love?

There is no need to blush; I do not ask
To wring confession from thee for thy sins –
I know how pretty maids can turn men's heads,
I know attention has a double edge:
In nine parts loathsome irritation
And one part a begrudging flattery.

Jen
Hah! Yeah, I know what you mean there. I have some
experience with guys, with men, they're . . . generally fine.
If that's what you're into. I'm actually mostly a lesbian.

Lady Kate
A lesbian? What sort of thing is that?

It is a religious order, like a nun?

Jen
Well . . . you could say it's a calling. Sometimes it feels like
I've taken a vow of celibacy.

Lady Kate

    I took a solemn vow before God too:
    I promised to love, honour and obey.
    I gained so much – this castle, servants and
    All the respect and admiration
    That suits a lady of my birth. I was
    The eldest child – my parents did not know
    That they would have my brother after me,
    Being advanced in years when I was born –
    So I was raised to think, to shoot, to write,
    To manage an estate: my father planned
    To make me his inheritor! But then
    My brother Edmund came. And do not think
    That I do not love him, or that I am
    Ungrateful for these things that I have gained –
    A husband well respected, gallant, strong,
    Advancing in the world! As he withdraws
    From me – but I, some days I feel the lack
    Of that which I have lost, most principally
    The future I imagined for myself.
    I am a wife. Now just a wife. Nay, no,
    Not 'just', I do not mean to make it small,
    It is a joy, a duty, I am blessed,
    And yet . . .

Jen

    It's tough when people see you only in relation to men.

Lady Kate

    Yes! That is what I mean, those are the words!
    I read Protagoras – for I can read:
    He wrote, 'Man is the measure of all things',
    But why 'man', why not 'woman'? Why say man?
    When hast thou seen a smith or carpenter
    Decrease in skill by practicing his craft?
    Why then do men insult the work of God
    Claiming all heavenly attributes for Adam,
    And leaving none for Eve, His second made?
    Was Athena the lesser for her sex?

Hippolyta not roused by that same Sun
As Hercules? Would Cleopatra's reign
Have been more golden still had she possessed
That which she lacked?[2]

Jen

Yeah! I mean, not 'yeah' it would have been better, 'yeah'
as in, yeah!

Beat. Despite having enjoyed voicing these thoughts, **Kate** *is still in
the same situation.*

Jen

It's tough. Like I guess women in the fourteen – uh,
women now – don't have loads of options. Like you can do
all that stuff and say all that stuff, but you still sortof have
to get married and it does have to be to a man . . . yeah,
just knowing what your situation is, is cool, and I don't
think you're bad or sinful or whatever for feeling
frustrated but you can't just fix the world by changing
your attitude, I guess is what I'm trying to say.

It's a bit of a fucking shitter innit.

Lady Kate

'It's a bit of a fucking shitter innit.'

Hah. I like the way thou speak'st.

Jen

Yeah?

Lady Kate

Yes, it's interesting. It's less . . . what am I trying to say?
One doesn't always have to –

Kate *makes a gesture halfway between a karate chop and a point to
indicate 'driving forward'.*

Lady Kate

Well, there is much to do, much to attend.

---

[2] i.e. a penis.

I thank thee for thy sympathetic ear,
And charge thee, on thy order, not to speak
To any other of what I confessed;
Keep thou my words in total secrecy
As if I spake them in that sacrament.
Be like a priest – be like a lesbian![3]

Jen
Like a? Oh, yeah, like a priest – gotcha. Yeah, I won't tell anyone.

Lady Kate
Go to thy duties then. And me to mine.

Kate *exits.*

Scene IX

Bangor

The scene changes around **Jen***, who watches it go.*

Jen
Oh heck.

She checks the map again but this time **Hotspur***,* **Douglas***,* **Northumberland** *and* **Worcester** *enter immediately.* **Worcester** *has a normal, non-magical map.*

Douglas
Come, show the map: we shall carve up the land.

Worcester
I have divided England equally:
All land from Trent and Severn hitherto –
By south and east to Mortimer is assign'd:
All westward, Wales beyond the Severn shore,
To Owen Glendower: brother, to you
The remnant northward, lying off from Trent,
Which someday you will hand down to your son.

---

[3] Kate still thinks lesbianism is a religious order.

So our indentures tripartite are drawn;
Which being sealèd interchangeably,
Tomorrow we set forth to Shrewsbury
Where we shall draw together tenants, friends,
And neighbouring gentlemen into one power.
And after that – *alea iacta est!*
The die is cast and we shall win or lose.

Douglas
What number can the King's power reach unto?

Northumberland
Some ten or twenty thousand, I should think.

Jen *approaches* **Hotspur** *and tries to get her attention.*

Douglas
Which nobles likely head the king's forces?

Northumberland
The Earl of Stafford, and of Westmorland,
Perhaps Prince John.

Hotspur
Perhaps the Prince of Wales?

Jen
Pst!

Hotspur
I hope he drinks his courage deep enough
To face me!

Douglas
Has he given you some offence?

Jen
Pst!!

Hotspur
His every step, his every word offends,
In breathing, yea, in looking he offends,
His cringing, whinging nature breeds offence.

Jen

> My Lord Hotspur, sorry to interrupt,
> Can I've a word? Verily 'tis important.

Worcester

> Soldier, you may but borrow my nephew,
> See to it that you do return him straight!

Douglas, **Worcester** *and* **Northumberland** *withdraw to discuss quietly.*

Hotspur

> Thou hast thy audience: what is the news?

Jen

> Uh, hello. We just spoke just now, you told me to fetch
> your horse?

Hotspur

> Thou hast mistaken me; I did not call.

Jen

> Just now we were in your castle in Alnwick and you asked
> me to fetch your horse!

Hotspur

> My castle is three hundred miles away
> And I have not been there for several weeks;
> If thou art making sport of me be warned
> I do not suffer fools and timewasters.

Jen

> You met me at Holmedon Hill, and then in London, and
> then just now in Alnwick, just now! I'm the girl from
> Framlingham, I shook your hand and then something
> happened, I think we might be connected . . . maybe . . .
> because we're both . . .

Hotspur

> Go to! Do not approach me, get thee hence!

Jen

> But I need to talk to you –

Hotspur

I care not who thou art or whence thou came
But get thee back there with expedience;
Thy face portends unwelcome happenings,
Strange sights and painful shocks, I say go to!

Jen

I'm trying to go to, I'm going and I'm toing! (*Trying to hint at something.*) I wondered if, maybe, you'd like to come too?

Hotspur

I have a kingdom that I must o'erturn,
A mission to fulfil, a crown to win!

Hotspur *goes to walk away.*

Jen

Your Dad keeps calling you his son!

She stops.

Your uncle calls you his nephew. Your wife calls you her husband.

Do you . . . do you really not know?

Hotspur

Know what?

Hotspur *goes back to join the others. Enter* **Sam**.

Sam

There you are sugarspice, found you at last!

Jen

Oh where the hell have you bloody been?!

Sam

We got caught on opposite sides of a transition.

Jen

Too right, opposite sides of a transition! Look, what's meant to be happening in this scene?

Sam (*looking at the map with her*)

Looks like the rebels are planning their attack. Hotspur and Worcester do some negotiating. Kate comes in and they have another argument and then that's it – we're into the interval.

Why is Douglas here, he's not in this scene? Where are Mortimer and Glendower?

Jen

I don't know, I don't know who Mortimer and Glendower even are!

Sam

What did you do?

Jen

Nothing, I didn't do anything!

Sam

Give me the map!

Jen *gives* **Sam** *the map back.*

Sam

No, no, this is all wrong. Mortimer and Glendower are meant to be here; Glendower has to exit and then come back on with Kate.

Enter **Kate**.

Sam

All right. Come on, we can skip this.

Jen

Hang on, wait – just watch!

Hotspur *and* **Kate**.

Hotspur

Good morrow, wife.

Lady Kate

Good morrow, my husband.

Hotspur

I feared you would not deign to meet us here
For what I said and how I spoke to you.

Lady Kate

Such warring words are poor ground indeed
To build a marriage on't.

Hotspur

I know none else.
Forgive me that I said I loved thee not
And called thee trifler, and raised my voice.

Lady Kate

I hear thy heartfelt plea, my noble lord,
And it has pierced my woman's breast as if . . .

Uh . . . I feel like I'm supposed to forgive you but, like, I
don't want to? I changed who I was to become your wife,
that wasn't trifling.

But I don't want to look at the things I left behind, I want
to look at the things we could have, together.

Hotspur

I am most moved by thy words, good my wife . . .
And . . .

Fuck it! I'm really sorry. I'm really, really sorry. I love you.

Lady Kate

I love you too.

*They take each other's hands. They kiss, and as they do there is
another big moment of magical connection. The house lights flicker.*

Did you feel that?

Hotspur

I did. I think I've felt it before, when I met someone . . . a
girl, up at Holmedon Hill.

Lady Kate

Did you kiss her too?

Hotspur
No! I shook her hand.

Lady Kate
When was this?

Hotspur
It was months ago . . . I think? Although it feels like it wasn't that long?

Lady Kate
Do you know something weird? I don't remember how I got here. I was in Alnwick talking to her, and now I'm here –

Hotspur
But you don't remember the journey.

Lady Kate
No.

Hotspur
Me neither. I've been from Holemdon to Alnwick to London to Wales and I don't think I've spent any time on the road at all, or if I have I don't remember it.

A worrying sound happens overhead, like big gears grinding or machinery straining. **Sam** *and* **Jen** *are the only ones who hear it.*

Jen
What was that?

Hotspur
Do you know what else is strange? When I was in London, I thought my father looked exactly like King Henry.

Lady Kate
They do look similar.

Hotspur
No no no, like they had the same face – I didn't even recognise Dad at first.

The big gears overhead grind again.

Sam

What is this; I've never seen this before.

Lady Kate

I think something's wrong here!

Hotspur

So do I. Do you know what else? I think we're being
watched.

The noise of the big machine really breaking down. This time **Kate**
and **Hotspur** *hear it.*

Lady Kate

What was that?!

We pick up **Worcester,** **Douglas',** *and* **Northumberland's**
conversation.

Worcester

I've just had a thought.

Here we are, planning to overthrow Henry Bolingbroke
and install Edmund Mortimer as King – but have either of
you ever stopped to ask like . . . why we even have a
hereditary monarchy in the first place?

Douglas

I've just had a thought as well – I wonder if my military
offensives over the last several years, although profitable in
the short-term, have perhaps contributed to a decreasing
geopolitical stability in the border region that actually
hampers my long-term goals? I think I'd have more success
pursuing a cooperative and peaceful foreign policy rather
than one requiring constant military victory and which
relies so heavily on projecting an image of toxic masculinity.

Grinding gears again.

Sam *jumps in, wielding the map to put everyone back in their place
and reinforcing the rhythm.*

Sam

My lords, my Lady Katherine, your beds
Are ready for you! Look, the hour grows late:

Will you come in? Tomorrow you must ride
For Shrewsbury and you shall need your strength
If you are to repair those grievous wrongs
That Henry Bolingbroke has done you all.

Worcester *and* **Douglas** *snap out of it.*

Worcester
Indeed, well said, good knight! Let's all to bed;
This heavy business must have dulled my mind,
For I was briefly carried quite away
By philosophic contemplation,
But there are many real things to attend!

Douglas
Indeed! We'll shortly rush unto the field
All harnessed with our weapons borne aloft!
O what a glorious victory we shall win!

Sam *starts to shepherd everyone out.*

A look between **Hotspur** *and* **Kate** *– she goes with the others.* **Jen**
goes last, making eye contact briefly with **Hotspur** *as she goes.*
Hotspur *and* **Northumberland** *are left alone.*

Scene X

Continuous

Northumberland
How is it with thee, son? Art thou prepared?
What was the matter twixt thee and thy wife?

Hotspur
She'd have me stay with her.

Northumberland
A happy home is well worth fighting for:
Secure and stable, something to defend,
To pass on to one's children, too, one day.

Northumberland *notes the sunset:*

Somewhere King Henry watches that same sun,
And in its slow descent foresees his fall,
For sure he knows he will not see it rise
More than a dozen times again in life.
I shall see my son rise to topple him.

Hotspur

I am no sun. I am the moon,
Reflecting but the light you shine on me.
'Twas your campaign that won King Henry's crown,
And your feet that did leave the deep imprints
In which I walk; if I wear honours now
I put them on by borrowing from you.

Northumberland

Not so, the country's eyes do look to thee:
In all the towns we go through men cry out,
'It's Harry Hotspur!' Not Northumberland.
I heard it rumoured that the Prince of Wales
Fled straight to France the moment thou marched out!

Hotspur

He does not have a reputation
For great prowess in military scenes.

Northumberland

Indeed. In truth, I pity his father.
The Prince of Wales cancels all filial bonds
In heaping ignominy on himself
And I am sure his father takes it hard.
To lose a child to war or accident,
Or any deadly shock – that is a hell
That I pray thou wilt never fall into.
But losing a child because they bring you shame
Must be a deeper still infernal pit.
The bitterest part of grief, its loss, is felt
But unlike grief, shame never truly heals.
The shameful child reminds one every day
Of their transgression, and in consequence
Their face becomes a murder or a rape,

A violation written in that flesh
That once was smiling, bouncing in your arms,
Now unwelcome and unfamiliar.
One's mourning clothes are worn invisibly,
For shame is hidden in the empty heart
And speaking shame aloud doth triple shame;
False smiles hiding tears fill up the days
Until – I am told, by most unfortunate friends –
The parent wishes their own child were dead.
I thank God for thee Harry. I am proud
To say thou art my son; I am relieved
To see a bloom of strength and fortitude
In thou that in myself, in recent years,
I have felt fading as my own sun sets.

Hotspur
Dad . . .

Northumberland
I will not always be here. None can choose
The hour that they must depart this life;
All we can do is ready those we love.
Before we march to Shrewsbury I will sign
The deeds of thy inheritance, my son.
Thy name shall be inscribed and thou shalt take
Possession of all legal property,
Including Alnwick Castle and its grounds,
That thy great ancestors, and thy father,
Have handed down the ages for thy hands.
I make an early gift of this to thee.

Northumberland *places a hand on* **Hotspur***'s shoulder.*

Jen *comes back in hurriedly reading the map, pursued by* **Sam***.*

Jen
What happens at the end?

Sam
Give that back, you don't know what you're doing!

Jen
    What happens at the end of *Henry IV Part One*?!

Jen *finds her answer on the map. She runs over to* **Hotspur** *and spins her around by the other shoulder.* **Hotspur** *and* **Jen** *look at each other. The mechanical breaking noise is heard again very loudly by everyone except* **Northumberland**.

Blackout. End of Act 1.

Act II

A Danish Castle

It's Hamlet.

Northumberland *is King Claudius,* **Hotspur** *is Hamlet,* **Kate** *is Queen Gertrude,* **Prince Hal** *is Laertes,* **Worcester** *is Polonius and* **Douglas** *is Cornelius.*

Northumberland
　Though yet of Hamlet our dear brother's death
　The memory be green, and that it us befitted
　To bear our hearts in grief and our whole kingdom
　To be contracted in one brow of woe,
　Yet so far hath discretion fought with nature
　That we with wisest sorrow think on him,
　Together with remembrance of ourselves.
　Therefore our sometime sister, now our queen,
　Have we, as 'twere with a defeated joy –
　With mirth in funeral and with dirge in marriage –
　Taken to wife: nor have we herein barr'd
　Your better wisdoms, which have freely gone
　With this affair along. For all, our thanks.

Hal, **Worcester** *and* **Douglas** *politely applaud the happy couple.*

Northumberland
　Now follows, that you know, young Fortinbras,
　Holding a weak supposal of our worth,
　Or thinking by our late dear brother's death
　Our state to be disjoint and out of frame,
　Colleaguèd with the dream of his advantage,
　He hath not failed to pester us with message,
　Importing the surrender of those lands
　Lost by his father, with all bonds of law,
　To our most valiant brother. So much for him.

The court minus **Hotspur** *laugh politely.* **Sam** *hurriedly enters, realises where she is.*

Sam

Oh Christ.

She exits. The Hamlet crew carry straight on without noticing her and **Northumberland** *produces a letter.*

Northumberland

Now for ourself and for this time of meeting:
Thus much the business is: we have here writ
To Norway, uncle of young Fortinbras –
Who, impotent and bed-rid, scarcely hears
Of this his nephew's purpose – to suppress
His further gait herein; in that the levies –

Jen *enters somewhere else, carrying the map, checks it, sees someone else coming from offstage and runs out. The Hamlet crowd carry on undisturbed.*

Around about the time **Northumberland** *hands over the letter to* **Douglas***,* **Sam** *sprints right across the space, straight through the Hamlet crowd who fail to notice her, and off again.*

Northumberland

The lists and full proportions, are all made
Out of his subject: and we here dispatch
You, good Cornelius, our loyal friend,
For bearers of this greeting to old Norway,

　　　　　　Sam

　　　　　　Give it back give it back give it
　　　　　　back give it back!

Northumberland

Giving to you no further personal power
To business with the king more than the scope
Of these delated articles allow.
Farewell, and let your haste commend your duty.

Douglas
In that and all things I will show my duty.

Northumberland
We doubt it nothing: heartily farewell!

Douglas *exits*. **Prince Hal** *keeps trying to speak here, and is cut off by* **Northumberland**.

And now, Laertes, what's the news with you?
You told us of some suit; what is't, Laertes?

Jen *runs on and talks to* **Hotspur**, *shakes her by the shoulders. No response.* **Sam** *enters in pursuit. They struggle with each other for the map noisily. Again, the Hamlet crew carry on as if they can't see it.*

Prince Hal
Your leave and favour to return to France;
From whence though willingly I came to Denmark,

Sam
Idiot! Idiot! Give it to me!

Prince Hal
To show my duty in your coronation,
Yet now, I must confess, that duty done,
My thoughts and wishes bend again toward France

Jen
Get off! Ow, let go!

Prince Hal
And bow them to your gracious leave and pardon.

Northumberland
Have you your father's leave?

Sam
Mine! Mine! Give it back!

Worcester
He hath, my lord:

Jen
>You're hurting me!

Worcester
>I do beseech you, give him leave to go.

Sam
>Give me the map!

Northumberland
>Take thy fair hour, Laertes; time be thine,
>And thy best graces spend it at thy will!

Jen *manages to escape with the map and runs, dodging between the Hamlet crew, pursued by* **Sam**. *They run off.* **Northumberland** *turns to* **Hotspur**.

>But now, my cousin Hamlet and my son –
>How is it that the clouds still hang on you?

Hotspur
>Not so, my lord; I am too much i'the sun.

Lady Kate
>Good Hamlet, cast thy nighted colour off,
>And let thine eye look like a friend on Denmark.
>Thou know'st 'tis common; all that lives must die.

Hotspur
>Ay, madam, it is common.

Lady Kate
>If it be,
>Why seems it so particular with thee?

Hotspur
>Seems, madam! nay it is; I know not 'seems.'
>'Tis not alone my inky cloak, good mother,
>Together with all forms, moods, shapes of grief,
>That can denote me truly: these indeed seem,
>For they are actions that a man might play.
>But I have that within which passeth show;
>These but the trappings and the suits of woe.

Northumberland
>   For your intent
>   In going back to school in Wittenberg,
>   It is most retrograde to our desire:
>   And we beseech you, bend you to remain
>   Here, in the cheer and comfort of our eye,
>   Our chiefest courtier, cousin, and our son.

Lady Kate
>   Let not thy mother lose her prayers, Hamlet:
>   I pray thee, stay with us; go not to Wittenberg.

Hotspur
>   I shall in all my best obey you, madam.

Northumberland
>   Why, 'tis a loving and a fair reply:
>   Be as ourself in Denmark. Madam, come.

Exit all but **Hotspur**.

Scene II

Continuous

As **Hotspur** *talks,* **Jen** *enters.*

Hotspur
>   O, that this too too solid flesh would melt
>   Thaw and resolve itself into a dew!
>   Or that the Everlasting had not fix'd
>   His canon 'gainst self-slaughter! O God! God!
>   How weary, stale, flat and unprofitable,
>   Seem to me all the uses of this world!

Jen
>   Wow. Mood.

Jen *takes out the bottle of Diet Coke, throws it at* **Hotspur** *and hits her in the head.*

Hotspur

Fie on't! ah fie! 'tis an unweeded garden,
That grows to seed; things rank and gross in – OW! Fuck!

Jen

What a shot!

Sorry! Hi – do you remember me?

Hotspur

I am glad to see you well!

Beat.

Horatio – or I do forget myself!

Jen

Oh bloody hell.

Hotspur

But what, in faith, make you from Wittenberg?

Jen

I didn't come from chuffing Wittenberg, I'm from
Framlingham! Look, my name's Jen, all right? We literally
just spoke about twenty minutes ago. I came here to tell
you something important –

Hotspur

I pray thee, do not mock me, fellow-student;
I think it was to see my mother's wedding.

Jen

Fuck's sake!

Hotspur

Thrift, thrift, Horatio! the funeral baked meats
Did coldly furnish forth the marriage tables!
My father! – Methinks I see my father.

Jen

Where?

Hotspur
In my mind's eye, Horatio.

Jen (*checking the map*)
Look – let me save you about five hours here: your Dad's dead, your uncle killed him, Rosencrantz and Guildenstern are wronguns, don't stab anyone through a curtain, don't be mean to Ophelia, watch out for the Norwegians and stay away from fencing tournaments!

This place, this world, it's not what you think it is. You're not what you think you are! This might sound a bit unbelievable but I think you're really –

Enter **Sam**.

Sam
Hail to your Lordship!

Hotspur
Marcellus, hello!
What make you from Wittenberg, my worthy friend?

Sam
A truant disposition, good my lord!

Hotspur
I would not hear your enemy say so,
Nor shall you do mine ear that violence,
To make it truster of your own report
Against yourself: I know you are no truant.

Jen (*to* **Sam**)
What are you doing?

Sam
My lord, I came to see your father's funeral.
I saw him once; he was a goodly King.

Hotspur
He was a man, take him for all in all,
I shall not look upon his like again.

Jen

Sorry, excuse me! Hi! Prince Hamlet, could I please borrow – what's your name meant to be?

Sam

Marcellus.

Jen

Can I borrow her? I'll bring her right back!

Jen *takes* **Sam** *into an aside.*

Jen

What are you doing?

Sam

Darling, I'm trying to fix your bloody mess!

Jen

You said these characters are just antibodies – they are not, she's stuck here just like us!

Hotspur *notices the Diet Coke bottle lying on the ground.*

Sam

Don't pretend you have the slightest clue what's going on here when ninety minutes ago you still believed you were married to an Ancient Roman! You need to sit down and think about your behaviour, duck egg! Everything was going fine up there till you broke it and now we've been kicked all the way down to the bottom!

Hotspur *approaches the bottle.*

Jen

So what? Let's just tell her the truth and then we'll all find a way out together!

Sam

The only way out is back up there at the end of *Henry IV Part 1*, which we now can't get to because one of the major characters is having an identity crisis! We're lucky we ended up in *Hamlet*; if we'd fallen into *Titus Andronicus* we could have been baked into pies!

Hotspur *picks up the bottle and considers it. A sudden moment of suspension, she gasps, realises the truth. And suddenly we're back in* **Jen** *and* **Sam**'s *conversation.*

Jen

I checked the map, I know what happens to her at the end.

Sam

Well nothing happens now because you've derailed the whole thing! What's meant to happen is Prince Hal proves himself worthy of the crown by saving his father's life and defeating Harry Hotspur!

Jen

She dies!

Sam

Hotspur ends up as the tragic foil for Prince Hal's transformation –

Jen

But she dies!

Sam

Dies nobly! Dies giving a beautiful speech about time and life and honour – would you take that away? Would you say, 'Hey, actually, all those things you think you did, all those accomplishments, that was all a lie! The people that love you, they don't really love you – they only love this character you're performing!' Do you think it's *right* to inflict that kind of knowledge on someone? Rip them out of their life? Cheat them out of their death?

They're here because they want to be.

Do you want to end up like that, like one of these dead-eyed zombie cunts?

They look at **Hotspur**, *who seems to be in a world of her own now.*

Sam

I've been down here a long time – a really really fucking long time. I need to get out. Do you know something? I

wasn't Cleopatra. When I woke up in *Antony and Cleopatra*
I wasn't Cleopatra, I was Messenger Number 7. I had one
line in Act 3:

'The emperor calls Canidius.'

That was my whole character, my whole world, one line!
It's not even ten syllables! Even if you really milk
'Emperor' it's still only nine! I said that line until I was sick
to death of it; I wanted to bash my brains out or jump off a
building – I was so, so, *tired* of being a minor character.
You at least got to be Portia – you got to stand up there
being beautiful and clever and have loads of lines; it broke
my heart to see that! That one line was all of everything I
ever got! Until one night I realised I'm bigger than this! I
deserve to have a bit of recognition and a bit of self
determination in life, don't I? I worked hard to get that
map and to get you out, and you, you've cocked up my
escape and you're taking everything and I don't have
anything left to give any more!

Beat.

Jen
I'm sorry.

Jen *gives* **Sam** *the map.*

Jen
I'm sorry, I got caught up in it. Let's go. It might not be
too late, maybe we can find a way back up and get to the
door. Okay?

Sam
Yeah.

Jen
Prince Hamlet?

Hotspur *turns, hiding the Coke bottle.*

Jen
I'm sorry I disturbed you. I just thought maybe you'd
want to come with us rather than stay here.

Hotspur
    To be, or not to be, that is the question,
    Whether 'tis nobler in the mind to suffer
    The slings and arrows of outrageous fortune,
    Or to take arms against a sea of troubles,
    And by opposing end them? To die: to sleep;
    No more; and by a sleep to say we end
    The heart-ache and the thousand natural shocks
    That flesh is heir to, 'tis a consummation
    Devoutly to be wish'd. To die, to sleep;
    To sleep: perchance to dream: ay, there's the rub;
    For in that sleep of death what dreams may come
    When we have shuffled off this mortal coil,
    Must give us pause: there's the respect
    That makes calamity of so long life;
    For who would bear the whips and scorns of time,
    To grunt and sweat under a weary life,
    But that the dread of something after death,
    And makes us rather bear those ills we have
    Than fly to others which we know not of?
    Thus conscience does make cowards of us all
    And thus the native hue of resolution
    Is sicklied o'er with the pale cast of thought,
    And enterprises of great pith and moment
    With this regard their currents turn awry,
    And lose the name of action.

Hotspur *gives* **Jen** *the Diet Coke bottle and stays onstage.* **Sam** *and* **Jen** *go.*

Scene III

The Rebel Camp Outside Shrewsbury

The scene changes around **Hotspur**, *who watches it happen. Enter* **Kate** *with* **Hotspur**'s *sword.*

Lady Kate
    Harry?

Hotspur

Kate?

Lady Kate

Thy uncle charged me that I bring thee this,
He bids thee put thy armour on at once:
Your powers are arranged at Shrewsbury
And soon King Henry's army will be here.

I just said it 'cause I'm supposed to! I don't know how I
got here, or how you got here! Harry, what's going on?

Hotspur

It's okay . . .You've been dreaming. I'll tell you what you
need to do – give me that, and then you walk straight out
of this tent, get on a horse and ride back to Alnwick.

Lady Kate

I don't think I actually even know how to ride a horse. I
don't think there are any back there anyway I –

Hotspur

Of course you do, how else did you get here?

Lady Kate

I don't know! I don't know! I don't remember anything
except when I'm with you, my whole life exists just to
facilitate you! Something's wrong, don't you remember
what we said at Bangor, and that noise?

Hotspur

It was just a dream, I told you. Ride home, Kate. It's fine,
just walk out of here and ride home.

Lady Kate

Are you even listening to me?! Stop ordering me around
all the time!

Hotspur

That is thy role! That is thy calling, Kate!
It is what God and Nature hath assigned;
It is not Woman's place to give commands,

It is not Woman's place to rule thyself.
I would be softer with thee if I could,
But this our war is forged of swords and mail;
No weakness nor no womanly gentleness
Can we allow to creep into our hearts,
And so thou must away. Thou must. Just go!

Kate *throws down the sword*.

Lady Kate
Fine. It's impossible to be around you like this anyway – I don't know how I've ever managed to tolerate it. Love – I suppose! I love you! One of you: the other one, the one who actually communicates! But – this one – no. I'd rather walk into that darkness over there and find my own way through it than stay here with you – Look at me! You've cut me in two as well, I'm discarding the Kate that's been acting as your spinoff, enabling this shit, I'm throwing her away. So I'll say goodbye and I'll say good luck but I'm saying it to Other Harry, wherever that person is, 'cause whoever this is, this character I'm talking to right now? Other Kate might have loved you but I don't.

Kate *goes*. **Hotspur** *is left alone. She throws the Diet Coke bottle into the wings angrily*.

Scene IV

Continuous

Enter **Worcester** *and* **Douglas** *with a letter*.

Worcester
Good morrow, nephew! I just saw thy Kate
Come by me with her eyes all veiled in tears.

Hotspur *picks up her sword and straps it to her belt*.

Hotspur
I sent her home. Her woman's heart did break
In being parted from me, but t'was right.

My heart doth burn to charge into the field!
The red hot breath of action roars in me!
Five hundred Cheshire yeoman have we, yes?
We shall arrange them up by Harlescott
The better to look down upon the field
And rain their missiles on King Henry's power!
The cavalry from Wales –

Worcester
Yea, yea, but first –

Douglas
This letter comes from old Northumberland.

Hotspur
A letter from him! Why comes he not himself?

Worcester
He cannot come: he says he is grievous sick.

Hotspur
I prithee, tell me, doth he keep his bed?

Worcester
He did, his rider said, four days ago
And at the time of his departure thence
He was much feared by his physicians.
We must amend our plans: I say withdraw.

Douglas
His absence lends better opinion,
A larger dare to our great enterprise!
Yet all goes well, yet all our joints are whole!

Worcester
I loath to crush that Spring in you, my lord,
With further winter words but here's more news:
The Earl of Westmoreland, seven thousand strong,
Is marching hitherwards; with him Prince John.

Douglas
No harm: what more?

Worcester

And further, I have learn'd,
The king himself in person is set forth,
With strong and mighty preparation!

Douglas

He shall be welcome too. Where is his son,
The nimble-footed madcap Prince of Wales,
And his comrades?

Worcester

All furnish'd, all in arms;
All plumed like estridges that with the wind
Baited like eagles having lately bathed;
Glittering in golden coats, like images;
As full of spirit as the month of May,
And gorgeous as the sun –

Hotspur

Let them come on:
They come like sacrifices in their trim,
And to the fire-eyed maid of smoky war
All hot and bleeding will we offer them!
We'll fight with them tonight!

Worcester

Good nephew, be advised; we must withdraw!

Douglas

You speak but out of fear and cold heart!

Worcester

Do me no slander, Douglas: by my life,
I hold as little counsel with weak fear
As you my lord, or any man that lives!
The number of the king exceedeth ours:
For God's sake nephew, we must all withdraw!

Hotspur

Before we rode from Bangor father gave
All deeds and rights of my inheritance to me.
All powers and authority.

He trusted me to be our family.
I am the latest in that line of sons
That stretcheth back through centuries long gone:
Each drop of blood in me doth bear that debt.
I'll play the part of old Northumberland
And you shall see his manly strength in me
Reflected as a blade reflects the sun.

Douglas

My Lord of Worcester, is this not Hotspur?
Why doubt you his prowess in leading us?
Have you no pride in him? Have you no faith?
If Hotspur says that we can win this fight
Then I shall stand beside him and not quail.

Beat.

Worcester

Pray, do not take my caution for a sign
That I am not proud of thee.
I am.

Thy life has run by in so small a span!
Why I recall, but yesterday it seems,
A little boy who stood not three feet high
And could not mount his horse! I picked him up,
I sat him in the saddle, gave him reigns;
He galloped off. And now he has returned,
Though I and that boy both have been transformed
By time, and I see now thou art a man.

Hotspur

Your love doth make me twice the man I am.
And if I fall, so falls the man you know,
With all these honours you bestow intact.

Scene V

Continuous

A trumpet sounds. **King Henry** *enters to parlay, followed by* **Prince Hal**. *Something is different about* **Hal** *– he's sadder, meaner, militaristic.*

King Henry IV
How now, my rebel lords! It is not well
That you and I should meet upon such terms
As now we meet. You have deceived our trust,
And made us doff our easy robes of peace,
To crush our old limbs in ungentle steel:
This is not well, my lords, this is not well.

Worcester
For mine own part, I could be well content
To entertain the lag-end of my life
With quiet hours; for I do protest,
I have not sought the day of this dislike.

King Henry IV
You have not sought it? Hah! How comes it then?

Hotspur
It pleased your majesty to turn your looks
Of favour from myself and all our house!

King Henry IV
If Hotspur's good deserts have been forgot
We bid you name your griefs and with all speed
You shall have your desires with interest
And pardon absolute for yourself and these
Herein misled by your suggestion.

Douglas
Do not believe this snake, this King of smiles,
Who knows but how to promise, not to pay!

King Henry IV
This must be Douglas, Scotland's hairy thane,
Though out of orbit, straying further south
Than Heaven knows you have a right to be!

Douglas
Your majesty should check the map again!

King Henry IV
Put muzzles on your dog before he bites
Or you shall answer to the crown for him!

Hotspur
We gave you that same royalty you wear!
And when you were not six and twenty strong,
Sick in the world's regard, wretched and low,
My father gave you welcome to the shore!
And when the lords and barons of the realm
Perceived Northumberland did lean to you,
The more and less came in with cap and knee!
In short time after, you deposed the king;
Soon after that, deprived him of his life!
Disgraced me in my happy victories,
Rated mine uncle from the council-board;
In rage dismissed my father from the court;
Broke oath on oath, committed wrong on wrong,
And in conclusion drove us to seek out
This head of safety; and withal to pry
Into your title, the which we find
Too indirect for long continuance!

King Henry IV
These things indeed you have articulate
With some fine colour that may please the eye
To face the garment of rebellion!

Prince Hal *steps forward.*

Prince Hal
In both our armies there is many a soul
Shall pay full dearly for this encounter,
If once they join in trial. Therefore Hotspur:
I do not think a braver gentleman,
More active-valiant or more valiant-young,
More daring or more bold, is now alive.

For my part, I may speak it to my shame,
I have a truant been to chivalry;
Yet this before my father's majesty –
I will, to save the blood on either side,
Try fortune with you in a single fight.

Beat. Everyone is surprised by this.

Hotspur (*nodding to ask* **Hal** *to join him in an aside*)
A word.

Prince Hal
What say you?

Hotspur
I say I want a word!

Hotspur *and* **Hal** *speak aside.*

Hotspur
You cannot offer this in earnestness.

Prince Hal
There is no art, no pretence in my words.

Hotspur
You are unschooled, junior in swordsmanship –
I say it not to goad you but 'tis true!
So what mean you by this? What would you do?

Prince Hal
No less than is expected by my King.

Hotspur
You do not have to do this, you can go;
Get on your horse and flee to France right now!

Prince Hal
Why baulk?
Has your bravado all been burned away?
Have cowardice and meekness claimed your heart?

Hotspur

Look, Hal, cut the shit, all right, just talk to me. We both
know if we duel you are going to die.

Prince Hal

If my words give offence then draw thy sword!
Is Hotspur turned so womanly, so weak?
I say, thou girlish coward, draw thy sword!

Hotspur

. . .What's happened to you?

Prince Hal

Presume not that I am the thing I was;
For God doth know, so shall the world perceive,
That I have turn'd away my former self!
In thy image I now create my life.

Hotspur

An image, nothing more, a thin shadow,
A mere player dressing as a man:
So much art thou – a fake, a counterfeit!
I'll rip thy honour from thee at the root!
I'll drag thee ten times round the walls of Troy
And make a trophy of thy battered corpse!

Douglas

The quarrel lies not on your heads alone,
Therefore, I say to arms! Sound every drum!

Drums. **Douglas** *draws his sword, followed quickly by everyone else.*
Everyone starts backing off towards their respective sides.

King Henry IV

Rebuke and dread correction wait on us!
We offered fair, yet now we'll set on you,
And God befriend us, as our cause is just!

Douglas (*shouting offstage*)

Arm, gentlemen, to arms and steel yourselves!

Scene VI

The Battle of Shrewsbury

Drums, battle sounds, smoke, lights, music, noise!

Sam *and* **Jen** *enter with the map, groping their way through the battle.*

Sam
It's close! The doorway's close, we're almost there!

They make their way off again, dodging out of the way as **Douglas** *runs in, pursuing* **King Henry**. **Prince Hal** *runs in and intervenes.*

Prince Hal
Hold up thy head, vile Scot, or thou art like
Never to hold it up again!
It is the Prince of Wales that threatens thee!

Prince Hal *fights* **Douglas**. **Hal** *is all fury and bloodlust. He beats* **Douglas** *into running off and pursues him,* **King Henry** *exits another way.*

Enter **Hotspur** *and* **Worcester**.

Worcester (*pointing offstage*)
The Douglas is pursued!

Hotspur
Nay, 'tis not him!

Worcester
It is, I saw him through the smoke, it is!
Our allies need our aid, come, mount your horse!

Hotspur
Nay, where is Hal? Where is the Prince of Wales?
I saw him even now! The Prince must die!

Worcester
Your rivalry can wait – they need our help!

Hotspur
  Without it I am nothing! Go, I'll stay,
  And if I cannot find him I will come!

Worcester *runs out.*

Worcester
  Hal! Hal!

Enter **Sam** *and* **Jen**.

Sam
  This is it!

Hotspur
  Get out of here!

Jen
  We can't stay here, it's too dangerous!

Sam
  No, this is the spot! This is where the doorway will be!

Jen
  There's nothing here! Sam, we have to leave!

Hotspur
  Go to! I'll cut you down! I say go to!

Jen
  But this is where you die!

Hotspur
  I know where I'm supposed to be!

Jen
  Girl! I don't think you do!

The battle noise abruptly stops as the house lights come up. The door into the theatre that the audience entered through opens and light floods in.

Sam
  . . .We made it . . . We made it!

They notice the audience.

Hotspur
Who are they?

Sam
People! *Real* people!

She approaches someone in the audience.

Hi. I'm Sam. What's your name?

The audience member (we hope) tells **Sam** *their name, and she is deeply affected by it.*

I'll see you soon, (*audience member's name*).

Sam *drops the map.*

I'm coming home!

She runs through the doorway and is gone.

Jen
Are you coming?

Hotspur
Where?

Jen
Out!

Hotspur
I can't.

Jen
Why not? She did it!

Hotspur
My uncle, my father, Kate . . . my whole life is here.

Jen
It's just a performance.

Hotspur
Prince Hal. Prince Hal is here – I have to –

Jen
It's just. A performance.

A pause. **Hotspur** *and* **Jen** *approach the door. But as they are on the threshold* **Hal** *enters, grabs* **Hotspur** *and pulls her back.*

Prince Hal
It's your line!

Hotspur
If I mistake not, thou art Harry Monmouth.

Prince Hal
Thou speak'st as if I would deny my name.

Hotspur
My name . . . is Harry Percy.

Hotspur *closes the door. As she does the house lights come down again and we are back in the dark world of the play.*

Hotspur (*to* **Jen**)
I am a son, I am a nephew, I
Am princely, I am mighty. I am loved!
And I am happy! Do not shake thy head –
I say I am the happiest man on earth,
For I have all that men can ever wish!
Go thou thy ways, foul thing, and nevermore
I beg thee, nevermore to visit me!
I say again I am the happiest man!

Jen
I'll find you. Look out for me next time.
We'll go together. I'll find you.

Jen *grabs the map and exits as* **Hal** *and* **Hotspur** *prepare to fight.*

Prince Hal
I am the Prince of Wales; and think not, Percy,
To share with me in glory any more:
Two stars keep not their motion in one sphere;
Nor can one England brook a double reign,
Of Harry Hotspur and the Prince of Wales.

Hotspur
   Nor shall it, Harry; for the hour is come
   To end the one of us; and would to God
   Thy name were now as great as mine.

Prince Hal
   I'll make it greater ere I part from thee;
   And all the budding honours on thy crest
   I'll crop, to make a garland for my head!

They fight viciously. **Hotspur** *is wounded.*

Prince Hal
   You have a speech now. You're supposed to give a
   beautiful speech about honour and pride and death. And
   then you go out nobly, and I get to be magnanimous.

Hotspur *spits blood and dies, not nobly but bitterly and face down
in the dirt.*

A beat.

A trumpet sounds, and **King Henry** *enters. He sees what has
happened.*

King Henry IV
   Thus ever did rebellion find rebuke.

Prince Hal
   When that this body did contain a spirit,
   A kingdom for it was too small a bound;
   But now two paces of the vilest earth
   Is room enough: this earth that bears it dead
   Bears not alive so stout a gentleman.

King Henry IV
   Well done my boy, I am proud of thee at last.

King Henry *approaches* **Prince Hal**. *For a moment it looks like he
might embrace him but instead he gives him an awkward shoulder
pat or a handshake.* **King Henry** *exits.*

Prince Hal *stays with* **Hotspur**'s *corpse. The world of the play
resets.*

Scene VII

London, Eltham Palace

Enter **King Henry** *for the opening of the play.*

King Henry IV
> So shaken as we are, so wan with care,
> Find we a time for frighted peace to pant,
> And breathe short-winded accents of new broils
> To be commenced in strands afar remote.
> No more the thirsty entrance of this soil
> Shall daub her lips with her own children's blood;
> Nor more shall trenching war channel her fields,
> Nor bruise her flowerets with the armèd hoofs
> Of hostile paces: those opposèd eyes,
> Which, like the meteors of a troubled heaven,
> All of one nature, of one substance bred,
> Did lately meet in the intestine shock
> And furious close of civil butchery
> Shall now, in mutual well-beseeming ranks,
> March all one way and be no more opposed
> Against acquaintance, kindred and allies.
> The edge of war, like an ill-sheathèd knife,
> No more shall cut his master. Therefore, friends,
> As far as to the sepulchre of Christ,
> Forthwith a power of English shall we levy;
> Whose arms were moulded in their mothers' womb
> To chase these pagans in those holy fields.
> But this our purpose now is twelve month old,
> And bootless 'tis to tell you we will go:
> Therefore we meet not now. Then let me hear
> Of you, my noble lord and loyal friend,
> What yesternight our council did decree
> In forwarding this dear expedience.

Enter **Jen**.

Jen
> My liege, this haste was hot in question,
> And many limits of the charge set down

But yesternight: when all athwart there came
A post from Scotland, leaden with grave news.

Enter **Hotspur** *pursuing the Earl of* **Douglas** *as before. No music this time.*

Jen
Harry Hotspur – or so you call her – fought valiantly against the Earl of Douglas. Because war makes men of us, or so she'd always been told, and because her father loved her for it.

Douglas
Lay on! Lay on ya wee and scrawny thing,
I've fought grandmothers with more strength than ye!

Hotspur *and* **Douglas** *fight some more.*

Jen
And she wasn't alone. She had Prince Hal with her, who had trudged all the way up from London to see if he could kill a part of himself as easily as Hotspur killed Scots.

Douglas *runs off.*

King Henry IV
Yea, there thou makest me sad and makest me sin
In envy that my Lord Northumberland
Should be the father to so blest a child,
A daughter who is the theme of honour's tongue.

Hotspur *hears the word 'daughter'. Enter an out of breath and out of his depth* **Prince Hal***, who stops to pant. He realises he can hear his father's words.*

King Henry IV
Whilst I, by looking on that praise,
See riot and dishonour stain the brow
Of my young worry.

I mean Harry. I worry. I don't want him to miss out on everything I've put aside for him.

Hotspur *approaches* **Prince Hal**, *but something's different now –* *nobody's convinced by what they're saying anymore.*

Hotspur

On your feet, Prince Hal.
These wars make men of us. Are you a man?

Prince Hal

A spent one.

King Henry IV

O that it could be proved
That some night-tripping fairy had exchanged
Northumberland's child with mine when they were born,
Then would I have his Harry, and he mine.

Wait . . . I don't mean that. (*He goes to* **Prince Hal** *and hugs him.*) My boy. I don't mean that.

Prince Hal

Are you Northumberland or King Henry?

King Henry IV

I'm . . . I'm Dad. Where are we?

Jen

Hi!

She holds up the Diet Coke bottle.

Do any of you recognise this?

Scene VIII

Brighton, The Real World, Present Day

Sam *is waiting for someone.* **Jen** *enters. They are meeting for the first time in a while.*

Jen

Hey!

Sam

Hey.

Jen

Really sorry I'm late – the train decided to just stop in Hayward's Heath for fifteen minutes for absolutely no reason. Fucking Thameslink! How you doing?

They hug briefly.

Sam

No worries. I'm alright. Good, yeah.

Jen

You're looking well.

Sam

Thanks. Yeah.

Jen

It's good to see you. You could have picked a nicer day for it mind.

Sam

Yeah the Boardwalk's usually really nice in summer; I guess the cold weather's still clinging on.

Jen

Yeah there were those couple of days last week when it was gorgeous and now winter's back.

Beat.

Sam

So have you been up to anything?

Jen

I'm all over the place. London based but I've been bouncing around – I got back from Belize last week.

Sam

Belize?!

Jen

Yeah! I hiked up to a lake called Five Blues – 'cause it's got five rivers running into it – and some howler monkeys chucked poo at me. I thought that was made up but it turns out wild monkeys really do actually throw shit at you.

Sam

Ugh!

Jen

It was fine! I just washed it off in the lake!

Sam

I don't think I could do that. Where else have you been?

Jen

Oh all over! I did the Caribbean first – as soon as I got out and got my life together I *needed* some sun so I got a job on a cruise ship, believe it or not!

Sam

Really?

Jen

Yeah! Really interesting people. Quite a few like us actually, we had a little on-board community. There was me, and one girl from Glasgow who'd been stuck inside *The Taming of the Shrew*, and a Dutch guy who'd been Duke Frederick in *As You Like It*, and one of the chefs had recently escaped from a dimension that was entirely *Phantom of the Opera*.

Sam

Just *Phantom of the Opera?* No *Cats* or *Jesus Christ Superstar* or –

Jen

Apparently not, apparently there's no interconnected Lloyd-Weber-verse down there, it was just *Phantom*. For eighteen years.

Sam

Wow.

Jen

Yeah.

Beat.

What about you?

Sam

Oh, I . . . I'm doing really well. I'm directing a play, actually! Here, in Brighton, at the Brighton Fringe.

Jen

Oh?

Sam

. . . No. Sorry, that was a lie.

I just . . . I came here.

Jen

That's cool. Peaceful. Seaside.

Sam

Yeah, it's . . . it's tough. It's like, now what, y'know?

I work in the pub. I come home, I sit around. It's very low-end: bottom of the country, bottom of the food chain.

Jen *does not reward this self-pity. Pause.*

Sam

I'm really glad to see you again. Thank you for reaching out.

Jen

Of course! I mean. It's whatever. You got out; I got out. All's Well That Ends Well.

Sam (*laughing*)

Don't! Do not quote Shakespeare to me!

Jen

Genuinely didn't even realise I was doing it, sorry! Oh, I brought you a present actually. Ta-dah!

Jen *produces the map and gives it to* **Sam**, *who is moved.*

Jen

It came in handy. It's not magic anymore but I thought it might look cool on a shelf or something.

Sam

Thank you.

Beat.

Jen

I'm meeting some people for lunch. Do you wanna come?

Sam

I'd better go and get ready for work.

Jen

Are you sure? What time's your shift?

Sam

It's not till this evening but, I've got some stuff to sort out in the flat.

Jen

Okay. Well, good to see you yeah.

Sam

Yeah. I'll send you a message, maybe next time you're in Brighton . . .

Jen

Okay. Yeah.

Beat. Bit of an awkward hug.

Take it easy!

Exit **Sam**.

Enter **Hotspur**, *now in modern clothes as a trans woman. She has a bottle of Diet Coke.*

Hotspur
Heyyy!

Jen
Hey gorgeous!

They embrace happily.

Looking good, gurrrl!

Hotspur
Thank you!

Jen
Where's the others?

Hotspur
They're just catching up. Is Sam coming?

Jen
I don't think so.

Hotspur *comforts* **Jen**.

Enter **Hal**, *now a stylish gay man, and* **Kate**, *both in modern dress.*

Hal
She in?

Hotspur
Nah.

Hal
Oh. Did you give her the map back?

Jen
Yeah. I invited her to come with us.

Beat.

Hotspur
Dad took a while to come round but he got there in the end.

Hal

It's not your fault; you offered.

Hotspur

It is hard to get used to playing a new role, as it were.

Lady Kate

That's life though isn't it; that's everything.

Jen

Mm.

All the world's a stage.

The End.

www.ingramcontent.com/pod-product-compliance
Ingram Content Group UK Ltd.
Pitfield, Milton Keynes, MK11 3LW, UK
UKHW020714280225
455688UK00012B/353